Maintaining Morale:

A guide to assessing the morale of midlevel administrators and faculty

by Linda K. Johnsrud, Ph. D.

College and University Personnel Association, Washington, DC

About CUPA

Established 50 years ago, the College and University Personnel Association (CUPA) is an international network of more than 6,100 human resource administrators serving almost 1,700 colleges and universities.

The Association promotes the effective management and development of human resources in higher education. CUPA provides a forum for the exchange of ideas through annual conventions, workshops, and seminars; annual research and analysis on administrative and faculty salaries, benefits, and other surveys and special study reports; and periodicals, monographs, books, and videotapes on topics of interest to human resource practitioners.

Through its national office in Washington, DC, the Association keeps its members abreast of the most recent judicial decisions affecting human resource management and communicates that information to members through columns such as "Legal Watch" in the semimonthly newsletter, *CUPA News*. Additionally, CUPA provides members legislative information through "Legislative Update" and "Legislative Tracker" columns in *CUPA News*. To keep members up to date on the latest benefits information, the Benefits Information Program, administered by the CUPA Foundation, supplies "Benefits Watch" columns in *CUPA News* along with *Special Reports* and *Benefits Alerts*, which are mailed as events happen.

The Board of Directors, composed of elected regional and national officers from CUPA member institutions, provides governance and leadership to the Association. CUPA offers seven types of membership—Institutional, Individual, Retiree, Student, Associate, International Associate, and Corporate.

To learn more about membership in CUPA or any of its publications, please call 202-429-0311.

Cover design by Gregory S. Byerly, CUPA
Typesetting by Erin M. Sweeney, CUPA
©1996
The College and University Personnel Association
1233 20th Street, NW, Suite 301
Washington, DC 20036-1250
Library of Congress Catalog Card Number: 95-83564
International Standard Book Number: 1-878240-47-1

Table of Contents

Preface

The decade of the 1990s has not been good for higher education institutions. Slashed budgets and cutbacks are the norm. Retrenchment and downsizing are not just paper cuts; they are realities for administrative staff and faculty on numerous college and university campuses. The refrain that 85 percent or more of operating budgets are personnel costs is all too familiar: cuts mean people. Hiring freezes, buyouts, early retirement incentives, and layoffs are the outcomes as institutions struggle to live within their means.

The majority of administrative staff and faculty ultimately will retain their positions but they face increased workloads and decreased resources. They also face public sentiment that has never been less enthusiastic about support for education and has never been more critical about the quality of the product. Administrative staff and faculty are being asked to do more with less and to do it better than they have in the past.

The current climate is demoralizing. Senior-level administrators are challenged to maintain services and create new initiatives with staff who, more often than not, feel unappreciated and overworked. Midlevel administrators are frustrated with their mid-level status, which in difficult times seems to translate into increased responsibility for the present and decreased control over the future. Moreover, they see little opportunity for future professional growth and mobility as units are restructured, consolidated, or eliminated. Many faculty feel as if their input is sometimes sought but rarely heeded. Some demand to play a role in setting academic budget priorities but generally eschew any responsibility for making tough decisions. For that matter, many faculty distrust the administration to the extent that they doubt the legitimacy of a fiscal crisis.

Morale is a major issue. There is no resource more vital to the quality of a higher education institution than its personnel. The enthusiasm, commitment, and vitality of the administrative staff and faculty are an institution's most important resource. It is no accident that such a large proportion of the operating budget is dedicated to personnel—it should be. Unfortunately, in tough times senior-level administrators may be so preoccupied with the decisions they face, they fail to recognize or acknowledge the effect of those decisions. Morale erodes. Some people move on, some burrow in, and some grouse. Individual frustration becomes collective malaise, and the institution suffers.

The purpose of this book is to explore ways for campuses to maintain morale during these tough times. The essential message is: if you want to know how people feel, ask them. But don't ask if you are not prepared to respond. Two basic assumptions underly this message. The first is that the very process of assessing morale can enhance morale. For some, this assumption seems counterintuitive; that is, it could be argued that if disgruntled people are given a chance to grumble, it simply reinforces their low morale. On the other hand, disgruntled people often believe no one cares. One way to show that the institution cares about the well-being of its people is to systematically assess their perceptions of the quality of their work lives. The second assumption undergirding this message is that there are ways to enhance morale that do not require large infusions of new dollars. The vast majority of administrative staff and faculty on campuses chose their professions for the love of the work and the collegial setting; they did not expect to get rich. Certainly institutions should do everything possible to protect and improve the standard of living of their staff and faculty. However, there are many factors, other than monetary, that contribute to morale. The task is to identify the factors that are most important to the staff and faculty on a given campus and attend to those that can be improved.

The following chapters outline a process for assessing the morale on campus. The process is straightforward. The object is not to vilify anyone or any group but rather to identify patterns across staff and faculty: "What about your professional work life makes you feel good? What makes you feel bad?" Obviously, campus leaders need to preserve that which is positive and do what they can to rectify that which is negative. Leaders can do a much better job, however, if they have accurate and current data relevant to their campus. The goal of this book is to provide a rationale and a blueprint for assessing morale as the first step toward improving morale, particularly during tough times.

Linda K. Johnsrud, Ph.D.
July 1996

About the Author

Linda K. Johnsrud, Ph.D., brings her background as both an administrator and a faculty member to bear on the topic of morale. She spent 11 years as a midlevel administrator holding positions in housing, student activities, career planning and placement, and affirmative action at three liberal arts colleges (Knox, Linfield, and Grinnell Colleges). After receiving her Ph.D. from Ohio State University in 1988, she was appointed to the faculty of the University of Hawaii at Manoa. She now holds the rank of Professor and has served as the chair of the UH-Manoa Faculty Senate and member of the Board of Directors of the University of Hawaii Professional Assembly.

Johnsrud has written extensively on work-life issues of administrative staff and faculty. Her previous work on administrative staff has centered on promotion, mentoring, and career mobility. Her work on faculty has sought to identify barriers to tenure and promotion, with particular attention to ethnic and racial minorities as well as women. She has published in the *Journal of Higher Education*, *Review of Higher Education*, *Journal for Higher Education Management*, *Social Science Research*, *Higher Education Research and Development*, *Higher Education*, *International Journal of Educational Management*, *To Improve the Academy*, and *CUPA Journal*. Johnsrud is a frequent speaker on campus and in the community and has worked internationally with colleges and universities in Guam, Korea, Japan, and Western Australia.

Acknowledgments

Writing the acknowledgment of one's first book is a humbling experience. Reflecting on all those who have supported and challenged my thinking tempts me to begin by expressing my gratitude to my inspiring senior high school English teacher. In deference to my readers, I will simply acknowledge the many fine teachers, mentors, supervisors, and colleagues with whom I have had the privilege of working and who have shown me the power of caring relationships.

I owe a debt of thanks both to those who have influenced my thinking and those who have directly helped me conceptualize and produce this book. I would like to acknowledge Ronald H. Heck, Mary Ann D. Sagaria, and Marie A. Wunsch for our engaging conversations about what makes organizations better workplaces. Ron Heck also graciously lent his considerable technical expertise to this work. Special thanks go to Christine D. Des Jarlais and Vicki J. Rosser who both went well beyond their obligation as graduate research assistants to help conduct our work on morale. The three of us, Chris, Vicki, and I, also extend our thanks to every member of the administrative staff and faculty who gave his or her time to speak with us and/or complete our surveys. Senior administrators of the University of Hawaii deserve recognition not only for their willingness to support morale assessment, but also for their positive response to the findings. I would like to thank Daniel Julius for encouraging me to undertake this project and the editorial staff at CUPA for its diligence and care. And finally, my gratitude and love go to the two people in my life who "maintain my morale," my daughter, Britton, and my husband, George.

Publications and Research Advisory Board 1995–96

Chapter 1

Morale:
What It Is and Why It Is Important

The morale of administrative staff and faculty is rarely addressed on college and university campuses. Although this neglect is sometime attributed to the cavalier attitudes of senior administrators, it may be more a result of the difficulty of dealing with the vague and complex notion of "morale." It is far easier to talk about what is affecting morale than it is morale itself. The next chapter examines underlying reasons why the current campus morale is so often described as low or negative or eroding, but since the point of this book is to "assess" morale in order to improve it, a common understanding of what exactly will be assessed is critical.

Despite frequently heard references to "morale," it is not a well-defined or precisely measured concept. Typically those commenting on morale have an intuitive sense that an individual's morale is 'high," or the morale of the staff is "low," or the faculty's morale has "plummeted." Such comments refer broadly to the *level of well-being that an individual or group is experiencing in reference to their worklife.* As sensible as this definition is, measuring a "level of well-being" in any valid and reliable way is a problem. This chapter begins with a brief review of prior research on morale and ends with the set of working assumptions that underlie this guide to assessing morale on campus.

Prior Research on Morale

Not too surprisingly, early work on morale focused on the military. Comments regarding the "morale of the troops" or the "morale of our boys over there" are commonly heard when U.S. forces are sent abroad. One student of the military contends that high morale is indicated by "the soldier's absolute determination to do his duty to the best of his ability in any circumstances."[1] In other words, it is argued that high morale results in high performance. In fact, the report concludes that the maintenance of morale is the most important single factor in war.[2] Another report traces the history of the military's approach to morale and argues that this battle orientation has given way to a peacetime definition that focuses on the physical welfare of soldiers as the basis of morale (e.g., better living conditions, more commissaries, etc.).[3] Even more recently the military has acquired a more businesslike orientation, and morale is equated with job satisfaction. Defining morale in terms of the soldier's satisfaction with his or her work environment, the report found that morale is significantly related to proficiency and discipline, particularly for those soldiers with extremely high or low morale. That is, high morale is related to high levels of proficiency and discipline, and low morale is related to low levels of proficiency and discipline. The report also suggests that shifts in the aggregate level of job satisfaction in the army as a whole may indicate shifts in its overall level of effectiveness. Thus, maintaining high levels of morale is considered vital for optimum performance.[4]

The evidence that morale affects performance underscores its importance to the military, but to define morale as job satisfaction is inadequate. Despite the appeal of equating morale and job satisfaction (and the relative ease of measurement), it seems clear that morale means more than mere satisfaction. Morale seems to be an umbrella notion that includes, in addition to satisfaction, attributes such as enthusiasm, commitment, willingness to work, and dedication to common goals. Such an expanded definition is more in keeping with the powerful role morale is thought to play in performance. Other researchers have followed this line of thinking to identify multiple dimensions of morale. For example, a study of faculty and department heads used three indicators to measure morale: degree of job satisfaction, involvement, and alienation.[5]

Other efforts to define morale have focused on morale as a personal attribute that is a function of the individual's life as a whole. For example, one researcher argues that morale is a psychological construct that includes dimensions such as meaninglessness, powerlessness, social isolation, self-esteem, happiness/depression, and optimism.[6] Although these dimensions would seem to contribute to levels of morale, their personal nature raises another question for those concerned with morale in the workplace: is morale a function of one's work life alone? Can morale on the job be separated from one's general life morale? Although there seems to be little research on this specific question, one national study of workers established a strong positive and reciprocal relationship between job satisfaction and life satisfaction.[7] This finding suggests the commonsense conclusion that how one feels on the job affects how one feels about life in general, and vice versa. Thus, when attempting to measure an individual's morale regarding work, the result also may pick up their morale regarding their life in general. Everyone knows someone who walks around with the "weight of the world" on his or her shoulders, as well as those who are incessantly cheerful and perky. Often those extremes in disposition seem to prevail despite their surroundings; that is, the "oh-woe-is-me" types stay down no matter how upbeat their situation, and the "everything is rosy" types seem undaunted by any negative happening. Despite the familiarity of these extremes, they are extremes, and most individuals fall somewhere in between with dispositions that respond, to some extent, to their situations. Classic research on individual behavior indicates that behavior is a function of the personality interacting with the environment.[8] This line of thinking suggests that to some degree morale is a matter of individual differences (personality and attitudes), and to some degree it is a matter of environment or the context in which one works and lives. To some degree morale is also a matter of how an individual with a particular personality reacts to a particular environment.

This interactive relationship between personality and environment not only complicates the notion of morale conceptually, but also has implications for policy and practice. Efforts to improve the workplace to enhance morale are limited to what is within the control of the organization. Those with the power to hire and fire do control who is employed within the organization, but beyond those decisions, they have virtually no control over personalities or how personalities respond to certain conditions. Organizations can control the environment or the conditions of work, however, at least to a certain degree. Most who have worked within colleges and universities would argue that there is a great deal that could be done to improve the working conditions. There are numerous work-related factors that affect employees' regard for their jobs and the colleges and universities that employ them.

A final debate in the study of morale that has relevance for organizational efforts to assess morale is whether morale resides only within the individual or whether it resides within the group as well. Is morale a psychological construct or can it be an organizational construct as well? Researchers disagree on this issue and have argued that morale is a property of the individual, a property of the group, and a property of both the individual and the group.[9] When morale is defined in terms of satisfaction, dedication, or enthusiasm, the individual nature of the construct is clear. On the other hand, when terms such as "esprit de corps" or a "collective affective response" of a group to its organization are included, morale sounds like a property of the group.[10] Finally, one researcher argues that group morale is the composite of the morale of individual members. Following the researcher's logic, it seems clear that the morale of an organization can only be measured by measuring the morale of the individuals within the organization.[11] The question then becomes: Is it appropriate to simply aggregate individual morale "scores" within work units and assume that it is an indication of the morale of the work unit as a whole? Is the whole only a sum of its parts?

Organizations may well be more than the people who comprise them. Recent work on organizational culture suggests that organizations have a character and ethos of their own.

Arguably, however, character and ethos do not exist in a vacuum; they emerge from the actions and interactions (past and present) of people within that organization. The value of acknowledging the culture of an organization is that culture has an effect on those who work within the organization. The culture of the organization would seem to have both a cause and effect relationship with morale; that is, existing culture has an effect on the morale of organizational members at the same time that the culture reflects the prevailing morale. This relationship suggests that the measurement of individual morale has meaning, in the aggregate, for work units within the organization and the organization as a whole.

Summary of the Research Findings

And so, what does research literature say about the concept of morale? Morale seems to exist; people believe it is important. Morale is not simple; it is a multidimensional construct. There are reasons to believe that morale exists both within individuals and within groups. The definition of morale varies whether the researcher views the construct as residing in individuals or in groups. Morale seems to be a functional construct; research has documented the importance of morale to performance. Employees seem to bring some degree of morale from their home and life in general to work, and they develop some degree of their morale at work from factors within the workplace. Finally, morale seems to have meaning as both a psychological and an organizational construct.

Working Assumptions

It is clear from this brief overview of the prior research on morale that any work in this area must proceed based on a set of working assumptions. There are important unanswered questions about the concept of morale that need to be addressed by those who dissect such constructs and create and test scales to measure them. For the purpose of this guide, however, it is important to establish the definitions and assumptions. As has been stated, the definition of "morale" used here refers to *the level of well-being that individuals or groups experience in reference to their work life.* Therefore, an individual's morale is determined by dimensions such as *satisfaction, commitment, enthusiasm,* and *sense of common purpose.* The working assumptions of this book include the following.

Given this definition of morale, administrative staff and faculty will share a sufficiently common understanding of the concept.

The assumption is that when individuals are asked to respond to questions about their morale using the preceding definition, they will share a sufficient degree of understanding to make the measurement meaningful. It may well be that some individuals include dimensions in their definition of morale that others do not, but the assumption here is that, in general, individuals share an understanding of the difference between high morale and low morale. It also is assumed that slight variations in the notion of morale will not affect the findings of a study because a precise definition is less important than the shared understanding that morale is an indicator of how people feel about their work life.

Whether morale can be measured precisely or not, the factors that administrative staff and faculty perceive as having an effect on morale can be measured.

The second assumption involves what is to be measured in a project—not only how people feel about their work lives, but also what about their work affects those feelings. In other words, it is assumed that there are aspects of their work that have an effect on their morale, either positive or negative, and that those factors can be identified. It matters less whether everyone agrees on a precise definition of morale and more whether patterns can be identified in those aspects of work that individuals indicate make a difference to their sense of well-being, either positive or negative.

Simply to measure morale, without understanding what relates to differing levels of morale, is relatively useless in terms of making a difference. To improve morale, patterns in the responses of individuals must be identified that suggest specific areas of change. The factors that have an effect on individual morale may be highly idiosyncratic; that is, for one person, it may be acknowledgment or recognition for what he or she has accomplished and for someone else, it may be salary.

Typically, however, administrators cannot respond to their employees in an idiosyncratic manner; rather, they must respond with equitable and fair policies that apply to all or that meet the specific needs of certain groups. Thus, administrators need to know what actions will enhance the morale of most of their employees.

Morale exists in individuals and groups.

Based on prior research, it is assumed in this guide that morale exists at both individual and group levels. Moreover, it is assumed that the morale levels of individuals can be measured, that those measurements aggregate within a work unit, and that they are a meaningful indication of how the work unit feels. One of the criticisms of measuring individual morale is that the measurements may not be stable; that is, one day an individual's morale may be high and another day it may be low. There are two safeguards inherent in this study relevant to this criticism. The first is that because morale has been defined as a multidimensional construct, it is more stable than if it was defined more narrowly. For example, if only one dimension such as satisfaction or enthusiasm were measured, it might vary dramatically over time and situation. The construct as a whole, because it is composed of a variety of dimensions, will vary less than the individual dimensions themselves. The second safeguard lies in aggregating the individual results to the group level. Individuals may vacillate in regard to their feelings, but taken in the aggregate, these variations even out.

Morale matters.

Finally, it seems worth underscoring that it is assumed that morale matters. This assumption is based in part on the evidence that demonstrates morale affects performance. The evidence supports what would seem intuitively to be true: people who feel good about their work perform better. Organizations, in this instance colleges and universities, need maximum performance from their human resources. Given the fiscal constraints common to colleges and universities, it is critical for institutions to make the best possible use of the resources they have. During periods of hardship, when high productivity is most needed, both individual and organizational morale may be most threatened.

High morale characterizes those employees who will help an organization weather tough times and give their best to their jobs. Low morale characterizes those employees most likely to grouse, to work begrudgingly, or to do the least work possible; they feel most alienated from the organization. Organizations are well served to do what they can to ensure the high morale of their employees.

Morale also matters because successful organizations know that their human resources are their most important resources for reasons beyond productivity. Organizations come to be characterized as good places to work, as places that value their employees, as places that care about their employees' welfare. When morale is high, turnover costs are lower; employees are less likely to leave because they are not happy or because the "grass looks greener" elsewhere. Recruiting and retaining personnel is that much easier when an organization has a reputation for good people management. Morale is contagious. The high morale of current employees is passed on to new employees and so is the low morale. It is evident from the foregoing assumptions as well as from the review of the literature on morale that organizations have a stake in the morale of their employees.

Notes

1. Baynes, J. 1967. *Morale: A Study of Men and Courage*. New York: Praeger, p. 108.
2. Baynes, *Morale*.
3. Wesbrook, S. D. 1980. "Morale, Proficiency and Discipline." *Journal of Political and Military Sociology* 8 (Spring), p. 43–54.
4. Wesbrook, "Morale, Proficiency and Discipline."
5. Lin, Shang-Ping. 1992. "Correlations of Perceived Power Discrepancies with Ratings of Faculty Morale." *Psychological Reports* 71 (December), p. 1015–18.
6. Doherty, J. 1988. "Psychological Morale: Its Conceptualisation and Measurement." *Educational Studies* 14 (1), p. 65–74.
7. Judge, T. A. and S. Watanabe. 1993. "Another Look at the Job Satisfaction-Life Satisfaction Relationship." *Journal of Applied Psychology* 78 (6), p. 939–48.
8. Lewin, K. 1936. *Principles of Topological Psychology*. New York: McGraw-Hill.
9. Wesbrook, "Morale, Proficiency and Discipline"; Doherty, "Psychological Morale"; Sherif, M. and C. W. Sherif. 1956. *An Outline of Social Psychology*. New York: Harper & Row; Zeitz, G. 1983. "Structural and Individual Determinants of Organizational Morale and Satisfaction." *Social Forces* 61 (4), p. 1088–1108; Lindgren, H. C. 1982. *Leadership, Authority, and Power Sharing*. Malabar: Robert E. Krieger Publishing; Robinson, S. E., S. L. Roth,, and L.L. Brown. 1993. "Morale and Job Satisfaction among Nurses: What Can Hospitals Do?" *Journal of Applied Social Psychology* 23 (3) p. 244–51.
10. Gal, R. 1986. "Unit Morale: From a Theoretical Puzzle to an Empirical Illustration— An Israeli Example." *Journal of Applied Social Psychology* 16 (6), p. 549–64. Zeitz, G. 1983 "Structural and Individual Determinants of Organizational Morale and Satisfaction." *Social Forces*, 61, 1088–1108.
11. Lindgren, *Leadership, Authority, and Power Sharing*.

Chapter 2

Campus Morale in the 1990s

When times are "good" we expect morale to be high, and when times are "bad" we expect morale to be lower. Generally the 1990s have not been a good time for higher education. Although the academic prestige and the financial standing of colleges and universities vary substantially, there are, nonetheless, commonalties in the pressures they face. This chapter will focus on three forces that undermine the morale of staff and faculty on many college campuses: reduced resources and restructuring, loss of credibility with the public, and increased internal conflict.

Reduced Resources and Restructuring

The recession of the early 1990s resulted in financial hardship at both public and private institutions. To understand the effect, the reduction in resources should be viewed in relative terms. The decline of the 1990s is felt all the more intensely given the growth in the 1980s. Despite dire predictions for the 1980s, in reality resources for higher education grew over the decade.[1] Enrollment growth was modest, growing 1.5 percent a year, while total revenues more than doubled. Moreover, the increased revenues came from several sources:

> State funding doubled, from $20 billion in 1980 to $40 billion in 1990—a real increase of roughly 25 percent. Federal funding for higher education, despite publicity about cutbacks, also grew, from less than $10 billion in 1980 to roughly $20 billion in 1990. This growth occurred in both major areas of federal support: research and student aid. Tuition revenues grew from $12 billion in 1980 to roughly $30 billion in 1990. Endowment income also rose as a result of a bullish stock market, increasingly sophisticated management of funds, and more aggressive fundraising on the part of both public and private institutions. Revenues from sales and services also grew.[2]

As revenues grew during the 1980s, so did expenditures. The most striking increase over the decade was in administrative expenditures, which rose more rapidly than most other types of college expenditures.[3] Between school years 1980–81 and 1990–91 at public universities, administrative expenditures per full-time equivalent student rose 26 percent when adjusted for inflation. During the same period, instructional expenditures, adjusted for inflation, also increased by 12 percent a student.

Expenditures must be reconciled with revenues. Each source of revenue that grew in the 1980s has declined in the 1990s. As a result, institutions have considerably less money to spend. Federal support of higher education competes with Congressional efforts to hold the line on the federal deficit. Although state funding has been a steady source of revenue for public institutions since the 1950s, states now have decreased resources as a result of the recession and increased demands on those resources.[4] Higher education must compete for state funding against the needs of K-12 education, social welfare programs, federally mandated health and environmental protections, and overcrowded and understaffed prisons. Similarly, local finances are strapped, which hits many community colleges dependent on local support.

The growth in tuition revenues in the 1980s can be sustained either by increased enrollment (less likely in the 1990s than it was in the 1980s) or increased tuition (not popular with state legislatures or the public). And finally, endowment growth is dependent on the strength of the stock and bond markets, which may have difficulty matching the unprecedented growth rate of the 1980s.

The growth in revenues in the 1980s was not uniform, however; it varied during the decade by geographic region and, consequently, by institution. Many campuses began serious retrenchment, which included the dismissal of faculty.[5] Although there are no data available on the total number of faculty laid off in the 1980s, estimates range from four thousand to six or seven thousand.[6] Given the relative growth during the decade, it seems evident that not all institutions involved in those early layoffs were responding to immediate fiscal crisis. Some anticipated future cuts; others were restructuring programs to increase productivity, prestige, quality, and competitiveness. The latter may well have been the most demoralizing for staff and faculty—that is, it is difficult enough to be eliminated for lack of funds; it is even more difficult to be eliminated by an institution engaged in, what some would label, posturing.

Layoffs continued into the 1990s, but strategies varied. Some layoffs and position eliminations were adopted as a quick means to balance the budget. As the fiscal strain continued, however, more institutions restructured, consolidated, or redesigned their programs as a long-term means to cut costs. More than half of the states faced serious financial deficits in fiscal years 1990–91 and 1991–92, and, as a result, have cut overall appropriations for public higher education.[7] Private institutions were not immune; they too suffer from decreased revenue growth.

Campus Trends, 1994 reported an easing of the "crisis" atmosphere on many campuses.[8] Seventy-three percent of public colleges and universities received modest increases in their budgets. At the same time, fallout from earlier cuts and continued pressure still is evident. Eighty percent of administrators surveyed noted that their institutions have tightened the monitoring of expenditures; 71 percent have reviewed the mission of their academic units and have increased scrutiny of academic programs; and 40 percent have eliminated academic programs during the last few years. Sixty-four percent of institutions have reorganized their administrative offices. Many campuses have reported increased class size and teaching loads as well as the deterioration of physical plants.

Decline in morale is not necessarily directly proportional to the degree of retrenchment, but rather to the way the retrenchment is handled. Debates on campus center around issues such as the reality of budget cuts, whether the administration is fighting cuts or merely managing them, participation in decision making, secrecy surrounding "hit lists," the virtues of across-the-board cuts (everyone gets hurt a little) versus selective cuts (certain programs or personnel are eliminated). These issues are divisive; they cause rifts in the staff and faculty; they splinter the institution into the "haves" and the "have nots." Those institutions posturing for the future are likely to cut some programs and reward others—a rational strategy that is meant to enhance quality and build morale. Unfortunately, such a strategy tends to build morale only among those who are rewarded while those who are cut, as well as those who fear that they may be next, are further demoralized.

One report examined the rhetoric and imagery surrounding retrenchment and noted the besieged mentality of those who face dismissal as well as those who feel vulnerable.[9] The report describes the language of war (e.g., those who are displaced, eliminated, those who are victims and perpetrators) as well as the deep emotion felt by all involved. Although the depth of the feeling is certainly tied directly to the budget slashing and program elimination, there are other conditions particular to the 1990s that contribute to low morale and the sense of being "under attack."

Public Disaffection with Higher Education

The public is not protesting the slashing of higher education budgets. Rather, the public is calling for greater accountability in higher education. Some also feel an arrogant, out-of-touch professoriate is getting its "come-uppance." Even strong supporters of education want to know why undergraduates so often are ill served, why faculty teach so few hours a week, why the cost of education has increased so dramatically. They read stories about the abundance of graduates who cannot speak, read, or write and they fundamentally want to know what public institutions are doing with their hard-earned money. Many believe a better job could be done with fewer resources.

Between 1965 and 1985 public confidence in social institutions, including colleges and universities, diminished.[10] As early as the late 1960s, the public began to question the ability of campus leaders to control student unrest. Since that time societal problems and economic conditions have worsened, and higher education has failed to provide the solutions the public seeks. The status of higher education further declined when a series of national reports in the 1980s criticized education from elementary through postsecondary levels and a spate of books disparaged higher education specifically. *The Closing of the American Mind* by Allan Bloom, *Profscam* by Charles Sykes, *Up the University* by Robert and Jon Solomon, and *In Defense of Elitism* by William A. Henry III are examples of popular books that roundly criticized the state of higher education.

Despite their tendency to oversimplify complex issues, those authors do raise legitimate concerns about the affairs of academe. The public has a right and responsibility to question faculty workload, administrative growth, the efficacy of tenure, and the relevance of research. They should demand accountability for undergraduate education and question the abundance of new programs, centers, and institutes that drain resources away from the preparation of undergraduates. They should demand ethical conduct, devoted teaching, and worthwhile research from the institution.

Some of the critical attacks on higher education are sensationalized to sell newspapers or increase book sales. Others, however, are justified. Those involved in higher education have not always done as good a job as they should; moreover, they have done an even worse job explaining the job they do. It should be no surprise that the public questions higher education's ability to manage its own affairs. Higher education has become the subject of ridicule in the media. Reports of research misconduct and misappropriated funds undermine the integrity of academe. The press has a heyday with national awards given for irrelevant and useless research. "Political correctness" has received so much play, administrators and faculty appear to lack the courage or clearheadedness to deal straightforwardly with conflicts over academic standards, curricular change, or social behavior. Stories of lowered standards, admission quotas, and grade inflation devalue the worth of academic degrees in the public's mind. Interestingly, the rhetoric of the 1960s and 1970s that accused higher education of being elitist has given way to the 1990s rhetoric that higher education is not elitist enough.

Administrative staff and faculty too often have viewed with disdain criticism from the public. Some have been condescending to concerned citizens and believe the public just does not understand the norms and standards of academe. This self-righteous stance has backfired. The public's insistence on accountability cannot be ignored when it comes tied to resources.

Whether the public is justified in its disaffection with higher education or not, it is demoralizing. The many hard-working, committed staff and faculty feel unappreciated and undermined. Those who have served their institutions for years feel as if their long hours of teaching, research, and service are being dismissed. Although much of the criticism is aimed at large public research universities, all of higher education is suffering the attack. Staff and faculty at liberal arts colleges, state universities, and community colleges are quick to point out the differences in mission, student body, workload and commitment to teaching at their institutions, but these distinctions are rarely appreciated by a public that feels its trust has been violated.

To be employed as an administrator of a college or university or to be a member of the faculty traditionally has been a source of pride. Those employed in higher education chose to be there, certainly not because of the salary, but because they were committed to the work and because they valued the educational setting. This pride is being challenged by a public that believes there are too many involved in higher education who have become self-aggrandizing, wasteful, and negligent. Those who "feed at the public trough" are particularly singled out for derision. This attack is felt more broadly than it is deserved, but it is felt, and morale suffers.

Higher education's loss of credibility with the public is a double-edged sword. It not only has a direct effect on morale of those under attack, but also opens the door for state legislators, faced with competing demands for limited resources, to feel justified in cutting public funds to colleges and universities. Even strong supporters of higher education who believe that cuts are short sighted and disproportionately damaging must, nonetheless, listen to their constituents. In this cost-conscious climate, the prudent legislator must balance the angry taxpayer against what many believe has become the bottomless pit of higher education. It is difficult to justify the spiraling cost of higher education. It would seem that higher education could manage on less and it is being forced to do so. But it is demoralizing to know that resources for higher education are being cut in part because it is believed that higher education does not deserve the level of support it enjoyed in the past.

Internal Conflict on Campuses

The pressures of reduced resources and a disaffected public are external pressures common to many institutions in the 1990s. Another factor eroding morale is internal: the increased level of conflict on campuses. Conflict is not necessarily bad. Intellectual sparring, criticism, and differences of opinion are the lifeblood of higher education. When staff and faculty are splintered into warring and distrusting factions, however, the conflict is harmful. One report cited that the faculty was suffering from generational gaps.[11] In interviews, the researchers found junior faculty anxious and overworked trying to meet unspecified expectations of productivity, senior faculty shunted aside as unable to meet the performance standards as applied in tenure and promotion decisions, and midcareerists caught in the middle wondering if they ever would advance given the escalating standards.[12] Today those gaps are intensified as early retirement incentives and buyouts cause faculty members to look at each other, wondering who will go or who they believe should go.

The conflict between the generations of the faculty is exacerbated in departments in which new faculty arrive with near paranoia regarding their research productivity and a fearful disdain for large undergraduate classes, student advising, and committee work. Senior faculty criticize newcomers' lack of institutional service and believe they are motivated by self-interest and a quest for disciplinary prestige. The new faculty members dismiss the senior members of their department as out of touch, stuck, unable to move if they wanted to; at the same time, they are dependent on senior members' support for tenure and promotion. If differences in research paradigms are added to the mix, the faculty members may have little respect for one another's research; in fact, they may not even understand one another's research.

On the administrative side of the house, similar gaps occur due to differences in age and experience. Entry and midlevel administrators seek mentors and sponsors as a means to advance professionally but often feel that rather than helping them, senior administrators are protecting their turf. On the other hand, those with long years of institutional service see the young as job-hoppers more interested in their careers than service to the institution. As budgets are cut and services are consolidated, ill-will grows around issues of priority needs and seniority. Many recently hired staff were recruited to meet relatively new campus needs such as service to ethnic and racial minorities and women, people with disabilities, the underprepared, and nontraditional students. Those new staff feel most vulnerable—and they probably are. Service to special interest groups competes with what are considered "essential services." After the cuts, a reduced staff is charged with meeting all of the needs.

Besides interpersonal conflicts, administrative staff suffer the anger of many faculty concerning the growth of administrative positions relative to faculty positions in the last decade.[13] Numerous positions have been created in response to federal and state mandates, new technologies, increased enrollments, and increased diversity. Although faculty may believe those are jobs worth doing, not to mention that those are jobs they do not wish to perform, faculty believe those jobs should not come at the expense of instructional positions. Administrative staff who have worked hard to create and establish programs to meet those needs feel unappreciated by faculty who complain about "administrative bloat." It is extremely demoralizing for administrative staff to hear faculty advocating cuts to *all* units of the institutions—except the instructional units.

Another source of tension for both administrators and faculty is increased diversity on campus. The increased diversity of the student body has resulted not only in additional special services, but also in controversy over admissions standards and quotas, increased gender and racial tension, and calls for substantive changes in the curriculum. Staff and faculty are divided on those issues; their divisions often fall along generational, racial, and/or gender lines. The administrative staff and the faculty in academe have long been predominantly white males, and the increased diversity (modest but significant) among staff and faculty has disrupted the homogeneity of units and departments. Faculty feel collegiality has suffered; administrators talk about the lack of teamwork and common objectives. Decisions by consensus are becoming rare. Academe is not as comfortable a place as it once was.

The tension bred by diversity also has become increasingly covert. The "politically correct" rhetoric has silenced much of the debate over issues that demand attention. Academic standards, hate speech and speech codes, sexual harassment policies and procedures, ethical conduct, curricular revision, criteria in hiring, as well as tenure and promotion decisions are all legitimate issues that deserve careful scrutiny and balanced judgment. Instead there is grandstanding, trivialization, or silence. Higher education institutions cannot afford to ignore the tough issues, but the current conflict on campuses is causing many staff and faculty to seek refuge in their offices—to "burrow in" and just do "their work." To find the common ground needed to move forward on these issues, staff and faculty must be willing to engage in the conversations.

The Effect of the Current Climate

The morale of many is too low to care. Reduced resources, public disaffection, and increased conflict are taking their toll. Administrative staff and faculty face threats to their well-being from both external and internal sources. Academe might be better able to deal with the external pressures if there were more unity internally, but that is not likely to be the case in the near future. Nor does it seem likely that resource problems will be resolved or credibility heightened with the public as quickly as would be liked. Those are issues that will be around for some time, and that is why it is vital to address the morale of those who must care enough to work toward solutions. It will take the enthusiasm, commitment, and energy of countless members of the administrative staff and faculty to weather the current climate and emerge strengthened. There is real danger to the future of higher education if the most critical resources of academe—its staff and faculty—are ignored at the very time their vitality is needed most.

Notes

1. Hauptman, A. M. 1991. "Meeting the Challenge: Doing More with Less in the 1990s." *Educational Record* 72 (2), p. 6–13.
2. Hauptman, "Meeting the Challenge," p. 8.
3. National Center for Education Statistics, 1993. *Digest of Educational Statistics.* Washington, DC: U.S. Department of Education, Office of Educational Research and Improvement.
4. *Digest of Educational Statistics.*
5. Slaughter, S. 1993. "Retrenchment in the 1980s: The Politics of Prestige and Gender." *Journal of Higher Education* 64 (3), p. 250–82.
6. Slaughter, "Retrenchment in the 1980s," p. 255.
7. Kerlin, S. P. and D. M. Dunlap. 1993. "For Richer, for Poorer: Faculty Morale in Periods of Austerity and Retrenchment." *Journal of Higher Education* 64 (3), p. 348–77.
8. American Council on Education. 1994. *Campus Trends, 1994.* Washington, DC: American Council on Education.
9. Gumport, P. J. 1993. "The Contested Terrain of Academic Program Reduction." *Journal of Higher Education* 64 (3), p. 283–311.
10. Alfred, R. L. and J. Weissman. 1987. *Higher Education and the Public Trust: Improving Stature in Colleges and Universities.* ASHE-ERIC Higher Education Report No. 6. Washington, DC: Association for the Study of Higher Education.
11. Schuster, J. S and H.R. Bowen. 1985. "The Faculty at Risk." *Change* 17 (4), p. 13–21.
12. Schuster and Bowen, "The Faculty at Risk."
13. Bergman, B. R. 1991. "Bloated Administration, Blighted Campuses." *Academe, Bulletin of the American Association of University Professors* 77 (6), p. 12–16.

Chapter 3

The Institutional Stake in Morale

It seems clear that concern for the morale of administrative staff and faculty is a critical and timely issue for colleges and universities. Nonetheless, little attention is paid to morale beyond the acknowledgement that "morale is low," and certainly few institutions engage in any systematic assessment or formal attempt to enhance the morale of their staff and faculty. This chapter argues that institutions have a significant role to play in building morale.

Traditional Neglect of Personnel

Despite the abundant literature that emerges from schools of business management and organizational studies, most colleges and universities have only recently taken to heart the advice to pay more attention to their personnel. In part, most colleges and universities have been loathe to draw parallels between themselves and the 'for-profit' sector, as if adopting a sound practice from business somehow sullies the noble pursuit of teaching and learning. The aversion to business has a long history in higher education.[1] It continues today as scholars decry the efforts, for example, to apply total quality management to institutions of higher learning.

Another reason for the seeming lack of concern for personnel has its roots in the traditional norms and roles of higher education staff. In the beginning, there were faculty and very few administrators. Faculty have long been known to receive relatively low pay and have poor working conditions yet hold an intrinsic love of their work. Faculty rewards came from summers free from teaching, opportunities to travel abroad, sabbaticals, and most importantly, the autonomy to pursue their own scholarly interests. It is well known that most faculty would choose their careers again if they had the chance and that most stay at the institution where they began their careers.[2] If individual faculty members were disgruntled with their institutions, they moved on. A certain degree of voluntary attrition is expected, even welcomed, by senior administrators. Given this scenario, assessing or maintaining the morale of faculty has not been a priority.

The administrative staff has a more recent history than the faculty, and its growth has been met with suspicion, even hostility. Historically, the few administrative positions were filled by faculty members for short periods of time or as interim assignments. Those faculty members could return to academic appointments when their administrative roles ended. The median number of administrative officers per institution in 1860 was 4; in 1933, it was 30.5.[3] As the size of higher education organizations grew, the administrative demands became increasingly complex and cumbersome and administrative ranks expanded. During the 1970s, the ratio of administrators to faculty became as high as 2 to 1. To respond to the external demands for efficiency, equity, and accountability during the 1980s, the number of administrative positions again increased substantially, a 62 percent increase from school years 1979–80 to 1989–90.[4]

Administrative tasks today require higher levels of expertise, skill, and training than in previous generations. Despite their level of sophistication and specialization, administrative staff members still serve in a support capacity. They provide the staff functions for the primary missions of the institution—teaching, service, and research. As important as the support functions are, they are secondary to the primary mission. As a result of their support role, administrative staff members are rarely given the credit or recognition they deserve—and certainly their morale has not been a matter of concern. Faculty continue to view the growth in administration as bureaucratic expansion that comes at the expense of teaching and research.[5] The faculty, who do the bulk of the research, tend to be indifferent to the quality of work lives of administrators; thus, very little research has been conducted on midlevel ranks of administrators. The result is that administrative staff members receive little positive attention within higher education.

Role of the Institution in Morale Building

Old ways die hard, but colleges and universities have much to gain by moving from "benign neglect" to active interest in the well-being of their staff. Although it is risky to encourage higher education to look to corporate America for direction, colleges and universities would do well to note the problems that leading companies face and the solutions they have devised. In 1991, the cover story in *Fortune* magazine featured the "morale crisis" of middle management based on a survey of 750,000 middle managers. Managers were characterized as angry, distrustful, stressed out, and scared. The recommended first step in confronting the issue was to "find out what people are thinking."[6]

There are colleges and universities in which employees' cynicism and fear have escalated to anger and distrust, a level that *Fortune* labels a "morale crisis." Others may be more fortunate, but few are immune from the sense of unease that now permeates higher education. For many senior administrators, dealing with the morale of their employees has a much lower priority than fighting off the budget slashing that can cost employees far more than their morale—it may well cost them their jobs. Senior administrators cannot be blamed for putting their energies into raising revenues, increasing efficiency, and politicking for public support. And certainly, administrative staff and faculty want their senior administrators out on the front lines fighting for the resources needed to maintain operating funds.

But administrative staff and faculty also want their concerns and opinions acknowledged. No one feels good about being ignored, particularly during tough times. Many institutions have undergone significant changes as a result of retrenchment and reorganization. Many have instituted cost-saving measures that have reduced staffing and increased workload. And many face further cutbacks. Such actions have an enormous effect on those administrative staff and faculty who are responsible for the day-to-day activities of the institution. Not only do staff and faculty need to be heard for the sake of their morale, but also their opinions may be invaluable as future decisions are made regarding scarce resources. Senior administrators are well served to know the concerns, attitudes, and priorities of those actively engaged in the work of the institution.

If senior administrators want to know how the members of the administrative staff and faculty feel, they should ask them. In fact, they must ask them. This argument is based on two assumptions. The first is that the very process of assessing morale can enhance morale. For some, this assumption seems counterintuitive; that is, it could be argued that if disgruntled people have a chance to grumble, it simply reinforces their low morale. There is an element of truth to this objection, and when employees gather around the coffeepot to complain and whine, it is tempting to remove the coffeepot. Disgruntled people often believe no one cares. One way to show that the institution *does* care about the well-being of its people is to systematically assess their perceptions of the quality of their work lives. The administrative staff and faculty of a college or university are an intelligent and well-educated group of employees who know their worth to the organization and believe that their morale should be a matter of concern to senior administrators. Most will welcome a formal assessment of their concerns.

The second assumption undergirding the argument for a systematic assessment of morale is that there are ways to enhance morale that are not high cost. The vast majority of administrative staff and faculty on higher education campuses never expected to get rich. They chose their professions for the love of the work and the collegial setting, but they do expect to be treated as if they matter. Most are bright and most work hard; they believe their concerns are worth the time of senior administrators. And their concerns are not all monetary. Their morale may be affected by factors such as their role in governance and decision making, the system of rewards and evaluation, or their confidence in the leadership of their unit. Some concerns may well be monetary, but administrative staff and faculty are realistic. They know that budgets are tight, but they also know that decisions about the use of scarce resources must be made, and they have opinions about the priorities for the allocation of those resources. They want to be asked about their priorities.

To argue that morale can be improved in times of fiscal constraint is not to say that resources are unimportant. Certainly institutions should do everything possible to protect and improve the standard of living of their staff and faculty.

The task is to identify the factors that are most important to the staff and faculty on a given campus and attend to those within the institution's control.

Need for Institutionally Based Assessment

It takes courage on the part of senior administrators to ask employees what they think, allow them to respond anonymously, and take seriously what they say. In fact, it may seem easier to acknowledge the issue of morale but to rely on national data sets or published reports of what is important to staff and faculty. For faculty concerns, there is current comprehensive information available. For example, researchers at the Higher Education Research Institute, University of California at Los Angeles, have created a national data base on the quality of academic work life. Similarly, the Carnegie Foundation for the Advancement of Teaching published a report, *The Condition of the Professoriate: Attitudes and Trends, 1989*, based on a national survey of faculty, and another in 1994, *The Academic Profession: An International Perspective*.[7] For administrative staff, the information is more limited and less current. One study, *Leaders in Transition: A National Study of Higher Education Administrators,* provided the first comprehensive data on administrators, but that report was published in 1983.[8] Other work on administrators tends to be case studies narrower in scope: for example, there is a study of midlevel administrators' job satisfaction at a large public research university and a study of the career mobility of midlevel administrators.[9]

National data sets and published literature provide an important starting point for the assessment of morale (Chapters 4 and 5 provide reviews of the literature on staff and faculty issues), but those sources are not adequate substitutes for institution-specific assessments. National studies identify national patterns but they erase institutional differences. Researchers may break their data out by variables such as institutional type or size, but what is unique to a particular institution is lost. Cases studies of other institutions provide more of what is idiosyncratic to the institution studied, but typically the researchers are more concerned with making a case for why their study is representative of similar institutions than why the findings might be unique. The findings of both nationally based and case studies are helpful in identifying general issues that may relate to morale, but only institutionally based studies can provide an accurate picture of the relevant issues on a particular campus.

An accurate picture is not the only benefit of an institutionally based study. As argued earlier, the process of conducting a morale assessment is also a benefit. Chapter 6 will describe the involvement of administrative staff and faculty in the creation of instruments that reflect their concerns. The involvement of those who will be studied plus the opportunity for each individual staff member to respond anonymously is good for morale. Asking the questions suggests that somebody cares about the answers. Publishing a technical report disseminating the results to the campus community further indicates that the feedback is taken seriously. Finally, and most important, action taken based on the results of the assessment will do the most to enhance morale.

Institutional Commitment to Act

In the preface, the essential message of this book was stated: *if you want to know how people feel, ask them. And don't ask, if you are not prepared to respond.* More damage than good will be done by an assessment that administrative staff and faculty see as a sham or a whitewash. One of the most common criticisms of those invited to engage in participatory management is: "Sure, they asked our opinions, but they didn't really listen to what we had to say." In this regard senior administrators walk a narrow path. Some will opt to forego assessment because they believe they will be damned if they do, and damned if they don't. It is true that assessment can create expectations that are not within the power of the administration to meet. At the same time, assessment will identify issues and concerns that administration officials are able to address. There are likely to be few instant solutions to morale issues, but an honest response to the results of an assessment can improve the communication between senior administrators and staff members, and an honest effort to improve morale is more likely to improve the climate than no effort at all.

The results of an assessment give senior administrators a place to begin. The results will provide an overall reading of the morale of staff members, but they also will isolate pockets of low or high morale. Administrators can learn from both. What seems to account for the high morale of some units or groups and the low morale of others? What can be done to alleviate those factors that seem most associated with low morale? Do those factors differ by work unit, age, gender, or race? What can be done to replicate those factors that seem most associated with high morale?

A commitment to act from those with the power to address the issues is the best insurance that a formal assessment will have positive consequences for morale. The commitment to act does not mean, however, that the assessment must be conducted by senior administrators or even initiated by them. The assessment can be initiated by any concerned party as a means to inform the administration. With results in hand, the pressure of good data can be used to urge the administration to act. Optimally, however, the assessment of morale is a joint effort launched by all those with a stake in the quality of work life at the institution. The participation of those most affected will ensure that the assessment has credibility; the participation of those with the power to respond will ensure that the results and recommendations of the assessment are not ignored.

The next two chapters discuss in greater detail quality of work-life issues that are unique to administrative staff and faculty as well as special groups such as ethnic and racial minorities, women, and part-time employees. The intent of those chapters is to review the current national research to provide a starting place to design an assessment that reflects the concerns specific to a given campus.

Notes

1. Veblen, T. 1918. *The Higher Learning in America: A Memorandum on the Conduct of Universities by Business Men*. New York: Viking Press.
2. Boyer, E. L. 1990. *Scholarship Reconsidered: Priorities of the Professoriate*. Princeton, NJ: The Carnegie Foundation for the Advancement of Teaching; Finkelstein, M. 1984. *The American Academic Profession: A Synthesis of Social Scientific Inquiry since World War II*. Columbus: Ohio State University Press.
3. Rudolph, F. 1962. *The American College and University: A History*. New York: Random House.
4. Grassmuck, K. "Throughout the 80's, Colleges Hired More Non-Teaching Staff Than Other Employees," *The Chronicle of Higher Education*, 14 Aug. 1991, p. A22.
5. Kauffman, J. F. 1990. "Administration Then and Now." In *Administrative Careers and the Marketplace*, ed. Moore, K.M. and S. B. Twombly, New Directions for Higher Education 18 (4), San Francisco: Jossey-Bass, p. 99–108.
6. Fisher, A. B. 1991. "Morale Crisis," *Fortune*, 18 Nov. 1991, p. 76.
7. Boyer Ernest L., Philip G. Altbach, Mary Jean Whitelaw. *The Academic Profession: An International Perspective*. Princeton, NJ: Carnegie Foundation for the Advancement of Teaching, 1994; and Boyer, Ernest L. *Scholarship Reconsidered: Priorities of the Professoriate*. Princeton, NJ: Carnegie Foundation for the Advancement of Teaching, 1990.
8. Moore, K.M., 1983. "Leaders in Transition: A National Study of Higher Education Administrators." University Park: The Pennsylvania State University, Center for the Study of Higher Education.
9. Austin, A. E. 1985. "Factors Contributing to Job Satisfaction of University Mid-Level Administrators." Paper presented at the annual meeting of the American Society of Higher Education, Chicago, IL.

Chapter 4

Administrative Staff Work Life: A Summary Review of the Literature

As faculty like to point out, in the beginning there were no administrators. When the first colleges were founded in the colonial United States, each had a president who performed all the necessary functions to operate. There were, of course, no faculty either. In those early days, presidents administered their colleges and did all of the teaching as well.[1] Slowly as teaching fellows were added (precursors to today's faculty), they took on most of the tasks of dealing directly with students. They served as teachers, advisers, and disciplinarians. The first administrative position to be created under the president was that of treasurer; registrar soon followed. As other administrative needs surfaced, it was typical to ask faculty to take on such assignments on a temporary basis.

Just as colleges and universities grew so did the need for administrative services. As organizations became more complex, the skills and expertise needed for administrative tasks increased, and slowly, the career administrator evolved. Some would see as a loss the service orientation brought by faculty to those roles, but what was gained was the level of professionalism and commitment brought by career administrators. At the same time, administrators came to expect more of their positions. Exploring those expectations is the primary purpose of this chapter, but first it is important to identify just who are the "administrative staff" and what exactly they do.

Who Are the Administrative Staff?

For our purposes, the members of the administrative staff are those employees below the senior officer level and above the civil service sector. One writer, in a classic work on midlevel administrators, dubbed this group "lords, squires and yeomen."[2] The writer argued that they existed between the royalty and the peasants.

Similarly, this guide is not speaking of presidents, vice presidents, deans, or any of the positions for which academic rank or tenure as a faculty member is required. Although those academic administrator positions for which rank or tenure is required are certainly administrative, those who hold them tend to be faculty oriented; that is, they retain their tenure in their academic department, they endeavor to maintain their scholarly pursuits in their disciplinary field and ultimately, they return—or have the right to return—to their positions as faculty members.

Members of the administrative staff report to positions such as presidents, vice presidents, and deans, but they may well have large staffs of their own. Specifically, this guide refers to those who hold titles such as directors, managers, coordinators, supervisors, advisers, assistants, counselors, and specialists. As such, they may work within any of the four traditional administrative divisions: academic affairs, student affairs, business affairs, and external affairs.

It is difficult to accurately describe the backgrounds and training of this diverse group, in part because of their diversity, but mostly because little research has been done on midlevel administrators as a group. The last national survey yielding demographic and descriptive data on administrators was conducted in 1981; and it included presidents and deans and excluded assistant and associate positions.[3] The profile of an administrator at that time showed remarkable consistency. Most were white males between the ages of 45 and 59, married, and had earned doctorates.[4] National data indicate that the 10-year period between school years 1979-80 and 1989-90 showed a 62 percent growth in midlevel professionals, which suggests it is time for another comprehensive survey to determine whether the profile has changed.[5]

Based on 1985 data, it is known that 65 percent of the executives, managers, and administrators employed in higher education were male and 86 percent were white.[6] It also is clear that administrators are well educated.[7] Based on a 1981 survey and a 1984 survey of two-year institutions, nearly all of the administrators had earned bachelor's and master's degrees; approximately half had earned doctorates.[8] And finally, it is clear that turnover is relatively high. In a study of administrators in 3,500 institutions, 25 percent of those in midlevel positions changed positions between 1987 and 1988.[9]

The significant growth of this group coupled with the high turnover suggests a group that is not stable, that is evolving and that may be suffering from its own growth. One report details a 26 percent turnover of student affairs administrators every two years.[10] A certain level of turnover is expected and healthy in organizations, but at what point is the cost greater than the benefit of "new blood"? And more important, for this report, leaving one's position may be one potential indicator of dissatisfaction or low morale.

What Do Administrative Staff Members Do?

Broadly speaking, the administrative staff provide the support services to the institution's primary missions of teaching, research, and service. More specifically, they assist in developing and implementing policy, coordinate resources and activities, supervise administrative units that support academic functions, and serve as liaisons to a variety of constituents such as faculty, students, business, industry, and government.[11] These employees serve as the classic midlevel managers; they are the "linking-pins" both vertically between layers of the organization and horizontally between units.[12] They often provide the information on which decisions and policies are based; they rarely make those decisions or policies, but they are responsible, in turn, for implementing them.

Another reality of midlevel administration is that the activities are becoming more specialized and the workload more demanding as enrollments have grown and the external demands on institutions have increased.[13] There are few generalists left. For example, the lone development officer who raised money has been replaced by a cadre of specialists: a director of the capital campaign, a specialist in trusts and estate planning, a coordinator of the town-gown campaign, and a manager of corporate gifts. At the same time, the expectations for the performance of the office as a whole rises with the increased staff size. The pressure to perform increases regardless of whether there are more dollars out there to raise.

What individual members of administrative staffs do depends greatly on the size and complexity of the institution at which they are employed. Nonetheless, the external and internal pressures confronting higher education translate into demands for optimum performance by administrators. Those holding positions in high-profile areas such as admissions, financial aid, fund-raising, information technology, or operations are well aware of the importance of their roles. As a result, certain issues that determine administrative staff members' morale are unique to their positions and roles within the college or university in which they work.

What Are the Concerns of Administrative Staff Members?

Before identifying the concerns of these administrators, it is important to note that over time midlevel administrators in higher education have been found to be generally satisfied with their jobs.[14] In one study, midlevel administrators reported the most satisfaction coming from opportunities to help students and staff and from the opportunity to act independently and to have an effect on one's organization.[15] In another study, satisfaction was most related to the degree of autonomy in the job and the caring atmosphere of the institution.[16]

These findings provide a place to begin in the search for factors that influence morale. Obviously, the reverse of the preceding findings is also relevant. Low autonomy and a noncaring atmosphere may result in low satisfaction. The general satisfaction reported does not mean, however, that one is satisfied with all aspects of the working conditions, climate, or organization as a whole. It also is important to look at those factors that detract from the job. Reviewing the sparse literature that exists on this group, there seem to be three areas that consistently are the source of frustration among midlevel administrators: their midlevel role, the lack of recognition, and the lack of career development opportunities.

The Midlevel Role

By definition, the members of the administrative staff that are described here hold midlevel positions. As mentioned earlier, they provide the necessary information for decisions to be made, but rarely are involved in the actual decision making. For example, the admissions staff gather the data relevant to the effect of current admissions policies on the actual recruitment and retention of students. That information is given to the director of admissions, who in turn reports to the vice president of student affairs. Changes in policy regarding admissions may be formulated and recommended by the vice president in consultation perhaps with the appropriate faculty committee. Any significant change in policy will require the approval of the president in consultation with other members of the senior administrative staff. Finally, the revised policy will return via the chain of authority to the members of the admissions staff to implement.

This example of decision making in the area of admissions is replicated throughout the institution. It is a typical, rational means of decision making within a bureaucracy. It is, nonetheless, the source of much of the frustration experienced by midlevel managers in most colleges and universities. Most midlevel managers know a great deal about their particular function but they rarely get to make the decisions most important to that function. As a result, they often feel as if they have no authority for decisions that are made, and yet are held responsible for outcomes. Extending the admissions example, if a change is made in admissions criteria, it is the admissions staff who are charged with explaining and defending it to prospective students and their parents. Moreover, if the final outcome is not what was hoped for, the admissions staff will be perceived as responsible by the rest of the institution. This position is tough to occupy and the reality of being in the middle when it comes to administrative decision making can indeed be the source of low morale.

The Lack of Recognition

What may be even worse about their midlevel role is that these administrators feel they are not appreciated.[17] They are asked to provide information to the decision makers, but those who make decisions do not seem to recognize their skill, background, or expertise. The midlevel administrators often feel as if they have no voice in the decisions that are relevant to their areas of expertise. They are a well-educated group who are asked to work hard in demanding areas but their efforts do not seem to translate into recognition for a job well done.

Similarly, they may wonder if they are trusted by their supervisors. Midlevel administrators are in positions to generate and control much of the information that is channeled upward for decision making. The supervisor who needs to understand the information may ask so many questions the midlevel person begins to believe that his or her accuracy, or worse, his or her integrity, is being questioned. For example, those in technical positions who generate data are often plagued with requests to explain, verify, or replicate their work. Although the supervisor may be operating from ignorance and/or a genuine need to know, the technical expert may perceive the interrogation as a lack of trust or regard for their competence.

There is evidence that midlevel administrators are a highly committed group and the majority are committed to their position and institution as opposed to their own career in higher education. According to one study, commitment tends to be related to intrinsic rewards of the job such as autonomy, pride in work, and opportunity to meet interesting people. Salary is not a significant factor—unless it is perceived as out of line with others. Similarly, the lack of other extrinsic rewards, such as recognition and appreciation, can undermine the intrinsic rewards—and the commitment.[18]

In addition, lack of respect for the hard work and competence of the midlevel administrators does not come just from senior administrators; it also comes from the faculty who rarely seem to give credit to those administrators who spend much of their time directly interacting with students and external constituents. According to one study, "faculty show little respect for administrators and resist accepting them as full members of the academic community."[19] The loyalty and commitment of most midlevel administrators to their institutions make the arrogance of some faculty all the more difficult to tolerate, particularly in tough times.

Lack of Career Development Opportunities

A persistent source of complaint from midlevel administrators is the lack of career opportunity and professional development available to them.[20] The lack of opportunity for advancement plagues those within large organizations. Promotion or change of position is considered the primary means of advancement for administrators and most expect to move within their institution.[21] Few administrators enjoy the opportunity that faculty have to remain in their positions while advancing through the ranks (from assistant, to associate, to full professor) with increased salary and status. Administrators must typically change positions to advance but the pyramid-like structure of the organization hampers such movement; there are obviously more employees who would like to advance than there are positions for them to fill.[22] Of course, a substantial proportion of vacancies will be filled from outside the institution, limiting opportunity within.[23] Further exacerbating the situation are the barriers between functional areas (for example, it is often difficult to move from students affairs to academic affairs) and between institutional types (for example, it is easier to move within a research university than to move from a research university to a liberal arts college). As one report describes it, "the administrative marketplace is characterized by ill-defined career paths, multiple entrance points, and lack of explicit criteria for determining mobility."[24]

When mobility is limited or difficult, it becomes all the more important to enhance professional growth from within. Unfortunately, opportunity for professional development for midlevel administrators also is limited.[25] Administrators indicate they want to advance their skills and learn new ones. They are interested in both improving their ability to do the job they have as well as gaining the skills and experience necessary to take on new and more challenging positions. In a chapter on how to plan for career improvement, one researcher encourages administrators to do it for themselves because so few institutions do an adequate job of cultivating the talent of their administrative staffs.[26]

The lack of opportunity for development often causes administrators to turn to their professional organizations. The increased specialization of administrative work has resulted in increased professionalization of administrators and, concomitantly, to the growth of professional organizations addressing each area of specialization. If administrators must turn to external sources for their growth and validation, colleges and universities may sacrifice their commitment and loyalty. Administrators may begin to see themselves as more cosmopolitan and less local—a criticism that is now reserved for faculty! The fact remains, however, that professional development is important, and if the institution does not attend to these needs, administrators will look elsewhere. Limits on release time and funding mean that relatively few administrators will be supported by the institution to attend their professional meetings, and this restriction can only be the source of further frustration.

What about Ethnic and Racial Minorities and Women?

Ethnic and racial minorities and women continue to be underrepresented in the midlevel ranks of administrators, although they are better represented there than they are in senior-level positions.[27] As noted earlier, based on 1985 data, 35 percent of the executives, managers, and administrators employed in higher education were female and 14 percent were ethnic or racial minorities.[28] Comparative data are hard to come by and, although these percentages *do* reflect an increase in the representation of ethnic and racial minorities and women since 1980, they fall short of parity relative to the population. In an examination of midlevel administrative promotions, ethnic and racial minorities and women were found to be underrepresented in high-level positions and overrepresented in lower-level positions.[29] Women tend to be clustered in lower-level positions in certain areas. For example, in admissions offices in 1987, women held 28 percent of the directorships, 50 percent of the associate directorships, and 66 percent of the assistant directorships.[30] Women also are more likely to be in student affairs or external affairs than in academic or administrative affairs. Similarly, minority women administrators are most likely to serve as directors of affirmative action/EEO, financial aid, or student counseling.

In a study of administrative promotion that controlled for education, experience, and prior position, gender was identified as a negative predictor of the salary, status, and responsibility accrued for women administrators; and worse, the effect of gender is cumulative over time.[31] In this set of studies, ethnic and racial minority status was not a predictor, but the overall number of ethnic and racial minorities promoted was very small.

The underrepresentation of ethnic and racial minorities and women and their slow movement into more senior positions means that the few who have moved up are the only or one of the few of their gender, ethnicity, or race. Their underrepresentation has ramifications for their performance and their morale.[32] It will take a critical mass of ethnic and racial minorities and women at every level of the institution before those few do not feel like tokens and do not feel the isolation, heightened visibility, and pressure to perform that is common when underrepresentation exists.

Clearly, the experience of ethnic and racial minority and women administrators within higher education differs in significant ways from that of their white male peers. To what extent those differences result in differences in morale is unknown. It is important to assess not only the relative level of morale of these underrepresented groups, but also the factors that have an effect on their morale. Although the work-life issues of midlevel administrators outlined in this chapter are undoubtedly felt to some degree by all, there may be differences for those who are newest to the administrative ranks.

Notes

1. Rudolph, F. 1962. *The American College and University: A History*. New York: Random House.

2. Scott, R. A. 1978. *Lords, Squires, and Yeomen: Collegiate Middle Managers and Their Organizations*. AAHE -ERIC Higher Education Research Report No. 7. Washington, DC: American Association for Higher Education.

3. Moore, K. M. 1983. *Leaders in Transition: A National Study of Higher Education Administrators*. University Park: The Pennsylvania State University, Center for the Study of Higher Education.

4. Moore, K. M. 1983. "Examining the Myths of Administrative Careers." *AAHE Bulletin*. 35 (4), p. 3–7.

5. Grassmuck, K. "Throughout the 80's, Colleges Hired More Non-Teaching Staff Than Other Employees," *The Chronicle of Higher Education*, 14 Aug. 1991, p. A22.

6. Touchton, J. and L. Davis. 1991. *Fact Book on Women in Higher Education*. American Council on Education, New York: Macmillan Publishing Co.

7. Twombly, S. B. and K. M. Moore. 1991. "Social Origins of Higher Education Administrators." *Review of Higher Education* 14 (4), p. 485–510.

8. Moore, K.M. 1983. *Leaders in Transition: A National Study of Higher Education Administrators*. University Park: The Pennsylvania State University, Center for the Study of Higher Education.

9. Blum, D. E. "24-Pct. Turnover Rate Found for Administrators; Some Administrators Are Surprised by Survey Results," *The Chronicle of Higher Education*, 29 Mar. 1989, p. A1, A14.

10. Sagaria, M. A. and L. K. Johnsrud. 1988. "Mobility Within the Student Affairs Profession: Career Advancement Through Position Change." *The Journal of College Student Development* 29 (1), p. 30–40.

11. Sagaria, M. A. and L. K. Johnsrud. 1992. "Administrative Promotion: The Structuring of Opportunity." *The Review of Higher Education* 15 (2), p. 191–211.

12. Scott, *Lords, Squires, and Yeomen*.

13. Austin, A. E. and Z. Gamson. 1983. *Academic Workplace: New Demands, Heightened Tension*. ASHE-ERIC Higher Education Report No. 10. Washington DC: Association for the Study of Higher Education.

14. Bess, J. L. and T. M. Lodahl. 1969. "Career Patterns and Satisfactions in University Middle Management." *Educational Record* 50 (4), p. 220–29; Solmon, L. C. and M. Tierney. 1977. "Determinants of Job Satisfaction among College Administrators." *Journal of Higher Education* 48 (4), p. 412–31; Scott, *Lords, Squires, and Yeomen*; Austin, A. E. 1985. "Factors Contributing to Job Satisfaction of University Mid-Level Administrators." Paper presented at the annual meeting of the American Society of Higher Education, Chicago, IL.

15. Scott, *Lords, Squires, and Yeomen*.

16. Austin, "Factors Contributing to Job Satisfaction."

17. Scott, *Lords, Squires, and Yeomen*; Austin and Gamson, *Academic Workplace*.

18. Austin, A. E. 1984. "Work Orientation of University Mid-Level Administrators: Commitment to Work Role, Institution, and Career." Paper presented at the annual meeting of the American Society of Higher Education, Chicago, IL.

19. Austin and Gamson, *Academic Workplace*, p. 57

20. Bess and Lodahl, "Career Patterns"; Scott, *Lords, Squires, and Yeomen*; Austin and Gamson, *Academic Workplace*.

21. Sagaria, M. D. and K. M. Moore. 1983. "Job Change and Age: The Experiences of Administrators in Colleges and Universities." *Sociological Spectrum* 3 (3-4), p. 353–70.

22. Sagaria and Johnsrud, "Administrative Promotion."

23. Johnsrud, L. K., M. A. Sagaria, and R. H. Heck. 1992. "Decisions to Promote or Hire: The Case of University Administrators." *International Journal of Educational Management* 6 (2), p. 20–31.

24. Twombly, S. B. 1990. "Career Maps and Institutional Highways." In *Administrative Careers and the Marketplace*, 18 (4), New Directions in Higher Education, ed. Moore, K.M. and S. B. Twombly, San Francisco: Jossey-Bass, p. 17.

25. McDade, S. A. 1990. "Planning for Career Improvement." In *Administrative Careers and the Marketplace*, 18 (4), New Directions in Higher Education, ed. Moore, K. M. and S. B. Twombly. San Francisco: Jossey-Bass, p. 47–55; Morgan, B. E. and B. L. Weckmueller. 1991. "Staff Development for the 1990s." College and University 67 (1), p. 81–88; Scott, *Lords, Squires, and Yeomen*.

26. McDade, "Planning for Career Improvement."

27. Moore, K. M. 1990. "Creating Strengths Out of Our Differences." In *Administrative Careers and the Marketplace*, 18 (4), New Directions in Higher Education, ed. Moore, K. M. and S. B. Twombly, San Francisco: Jossey-Bass, p. 89–98.

28. Touchton and Davis, *Fact Book*.

29. Sagaria and Johnsrud, "Administrative Promotion."

30. Touchton and Davis, *Fact Book*.

31. Johnsrud, L. K. 1991. "Gender and Returns to Promotion: The Role of Social Relations and Power." *Social Science Research* 20 (4), p. 369–96; Johnsrud, L. K. and R. H. Heck. 1994. "Administrative Promotions within a University: The Cumulative Impact of Gender." *The Journal of Higher Education* 65 (1), p. 23–44.

32. Kanter, R. M. 1977. *Men and Women of the Corporation*. New York: Basic Books Moore, "Creating Strengths Out of Our Differences."

Chapter 5

Faculty Work Life:
A Summary Review of the Literature

There is a real danger in attempting to describe the "work life of faculty" as if "the faculty" constituted a homogeneous group. As one researcher concludes in a metaanalysis of research on faculty: "to attempt to generalize about faculty as a group except in the broadest possible way may be neither intellectually defensible nor operationally useful."[1] The primary differences among faculty that seem to differentiate their work lives are the type of institution at which they are employed (e.g., research, liberal arts, or community college) and the discipline in which they were trained (broadly: the humanities, natural sciences, social sciences, or the professions). The difficulty of generalization across all faculty underscores the thesis of this book: individual institutions need to assess the morale of each group on their campus. As argued here, morale needs to be measured in context, and most definitely, it would seem, in regard to faculty. Given that caveat, the purpose of this chapter is, nonetheless, to summarize the literature on faculty and their work lives to identify those current issues likely to affect morale.

Who Are 'The Faculty' and How Do They Differ?

The primary missions of higher education—teaching, research, and service—are the responsibility of the faculty. Simply stated, faculty are to transmit knowledge, create knowledge, and apply that knowledge to the needs of the society. This traditional depiction of their role obscures diverse obligations (grant-writing, advising, mentoring, curricula development, committee work, campus governance, community service, to name a few), all of which vary by institutional type and disciplinary affiliation. Before sorting these differences, there are certain broad demographics that do describe faculty as a group.

National data from 1987 on *all* full-time college professors indicate that of the 489,000 faculty members, 38 percent are employed at research or doctoral-granting institutions, 26 percent at comprehensives, 8 percent at liberal arts colleges, and 19 percent at community colleges.[2] Of this total group, 73 percent are men, 90 percent are white, and 51 percent are between 40 and 54 years of age. Of those employed at research or doctoral-granting institutions, 72 percent indicate that the highest academic degree they have attained is a doctorate. At two-year institutions, 62 percent indicate that the highest academic degree they have attained is a master's degree. Similarly, salaries range from a median of $68,700 for a full professor at a doctoral university to $48,670 for a full professor at a two-year institution. Overall, 33 percent of full-time faculty are full professors, although this percentage varies from 45 percent at public research universities to 16 percent at public two-year institutions.

Differences in institutional type result in significant differences in mission, and consequently, in the priorities of faculty members' work. The three-fold mission of research, teaching, and service is primarily the responsibility of the research and doctoral granting universities, while teaching and service tend to be the emphases of the comprehensive, liberal arts, and two-year institutions. The reward system for faculty, that is, the system of tenure and promotion, reflects the mission and priorities of the institutional type at which they are employed. For example, 66 percent of the faculty at research universities indicate that their interests are primarily in research or lean toward research.[3] On the other hand, 77 percent of those faculty employed at comprehensive institutions, 83 percent of those at liberal arts colleges, and 93 percent of those at two-year institutions indicate that their interests are primarily in teaching or lean toward teaching. Although untenured faculty may feel pressured to perform at exemplary levels in all areas, those at the research and doctoral granting universities feel the pressure to publish most acutely, while those at liberal arts colleges and two-year institutions feel the pressure to teach well. Faculty at those institutions with the least well-defined missions probably experience the most ambiguity relative to their role and priorities. For example, one research team suggests that high faculty morale in liberal arts colleges is related to the degree to which faculty identify with the mission of their institution and the extent to which their own goals are congruent with institutional goals.[4]

The work life of individual faculty members also differs significantly by disciplinary affiliation, a fact that is rarely addressed in research on faculty.[5] One researcher grouped the disciplines into four intellectual clusters labeled: hard-pure or the pure sciences (e.g., physics); soft-pure or the humanities (e.g., history) and pure social sciences (e.g., anthropology); hard-applied or technologies (e.g., mechanical engineering); and soft-applied or applied social sciences (e.g., education).[6] Another researcher builds on this grouping and describes inherent differences, including status, support for research, team versus individual research, scholarly products, links to industry, competitiveness of students, instructional techniques— even the role of the department head.[7] Those intellectual clusters are further characterized as distinct academic tribes within the institution's culture, tribes that make real differences in the expectations and priorities of the faculty who work within them.[8]

What Are Issues That Affect the Quality of Work Life for Faculty?

Despite the many distinctions that can be drawn among faculty, there are commonalties to the faculty role, and thus, generalizations that can be made about sources of faculty satisfaction and dissatisfaction. First, it is important to note that, just as most administrators indicate an overall satisfaction with their jobs, faculty for the most part love what they do. The great majority say that, if they had it to do over again, they would become academics.[9] They report a high degree of satisfaction with their intellectual lives, their courses, and their relationships with colleagues. Similarly, in a 1986 qualitative study of faculty morale, researchers reported that faculty were a dedicated group and that the intrinsic satisfactions of their work were rewarding and important to them.[10] Nonetheless, faculty in that study also were described as dispirited, fragmented, and devalued. Faculty indicate satisfaction with their profession but frustration with their institutions, particularly with what they perceive as incompetent leadership, poor communication with administrators, and lack of influence in the governance of their institutions.[11]

Despite the appeal of the faculty job, faculty are worried. The rewards for their jobs are eroding; their autonomy to define their work priorities is under attack; and they do not see the current leadership or system of governance capable of protecting their personal and professional interests. Each of these concerns may ultimately have a negative effect on the performance and morale of faculty.

The Erosion of Their Salary, Working Conditions, and Status

According to one salary survey, academic salaries of college and university professors at all ranks rose 3.0 percent between school years 1992–93 and 1993–94.[12] Adjusted for the percentage change in the consumer price index, this constitutes a real increase of 0.3 percent. This increase essentially reflects a pattern over the past three academic years. Relatively speaking, this information is the good news, compared with the fact that faculty lost ground for 10 consecutive years (from school years 1972–73 through 1981–82). At a rate of 0.3 percent increase per year, it will be years, however, before faculty recoup the losses of the earlier period. Salary alone does not act as a long-term motivator.[13] Nonetheless, salaries that are perceived as being unfair lead to long-term dissatisfaction and can have a great effect on the faculty members' morale and effectiveness.

Faculty complain about low salaries, but they also note the poor working conditions, such as inadequate facilities, supplies, and support personnel, as well as the deterioration of the physical plants of colleges and universities.[14] Sources of support for research and teaching vary dramatically from campus to campus, department to department, and faculty member to faculty member. Lack of resources such as graduate assistants, library services, computing support, even parking can be a source of real frustration, particularly if the resources are seen as inequitably distributed. Researchers report that although budget cutbacks influence overall faculty's morale, perceived inequities created by the cuts have the greatest effect on individual morale.[15]

Inequities exist not only among instructional units, but also between administrative and instructional budgets. The overall cost of higher education has certainly increased, but the most dramatic growth in positions since the mid-1970s has been in the administrative ranks. For example, between 1975 and 1985 the number of full-time faculty employed at colleges and universities increased by 5.9 percent. During that same time period, "executive, administrative, and managerial employees" increased by 17.9 percent and "other professionals" by 61.1 percent.[16] Moreover, the actual increase in the cost of administration is not always apparent. One researcher contends that some of the increase is obscured because it has occurred within academic units rather than in central administration. In other words, an enlarged dean's staff may appear as an instructional cost rather than as an administrative cost.[17]

Salary, staffing, working conditions, and the resources necessary for one's work are all tangible commodities that affect how appreciated and supported faculty feel at their institution. A more intangible commodity, however, is the esteem of the public, and in the long run, its loss may take the greatest toll. Numerous leaders in higher education have called attention to the erosion of public confidence.[18] Actual measurement of public confidence is rare, but there is no doubt that the perception of decline is real. Faculty are not immune to the fact that their role, their priorities, and their performance are being called into question. In a survey, which included faculty from 14 countries with well-developed systems of higher education, the majority of faculty in *every* country perceived that respect for academics is declining.[19] Among U.S. faculty, 64 percent agreed with the statement that respect is declining. As discussed at some length in Chapter 2 of this guide, the public wants to know how faculty spend their time, how relevant their research is, and how much they care about undergraduate education and the needs of society. These are tough questions for faculty to answer. These questions also portend a loss of autonomy that strikes at the core of the academic profession.

The Changing Nature of Academic Work

One of the overriding sources of satisfaction for academics is their autonomy.[20] Faculty are free to determine what and how they teach, the topic and method of their research, and the nature of their service. Moreover, faculty control their time. Beyond their course schedule and office hours, they determine how they spend their time, and typically where they spend it. As public demands for accountability increase, the autonomy of faculty to determine their priorities is endangered.

The demand for accountability is most evident in the increased attention to faculty workload. Workload studies are being conducted on numerous campuses, some administratively initiated, some mandated by state legislatures.[21] The motivation seems less the perception that faculty are not working hard enough (although it is often mentioned how few hours are spent in the classroom), and more that they are giving priority to the wrong tasks. Faculty do spend long hours working; the reported range is between 52 and 57 hours on average per week at public institutions.[22] Interestingly, the same source indicates that at *all* institutions, faculty spend 56 percent of their time on teaching activities and only 16 percent on activities related to research. Even at public research universities, 43 percent of faculty effort is spent on teaching and 29 percent is spent on research. Whether the overall time spent on teaching has declined is a matter of debate with some suggesting that it has, and others arguing that given a 20-year span, actual hours spent in teaching and preparation for teaching have been stable.[23] In fact, one researcher demonstrates that among undergraduate faculty at two- and four-year colleges, the proportion of faculty reporting substantial amounts of time teaching and preparation for teaching has markedly increased.[24]

The traditional reward system in colleges and universities reinforces faculty priorities—and faculty priorities determine the reward system. Although once tenured individual faculty are free to determine their own agenda, the process of socialization toward tenure is powerful. At research universities faculty spend five to six years establishing their line of inquiry, and they expect to pursue those research interests (or a variation thereof) through their next promotion. Nonetheless, many faculty criticize the reward system on their respective campuses as skewed too heavily toward research.[25] One-half of the faculty at research and doctorate-granting institutions agree (or agree with reservations) that the pressure to publish reduces the quality of teaching at their university. Concomitantly, 65 percent believe that there are better ways to evaluate the scholarly performance of faculty.

It is, however, the faculty who determine and apply the criteria in faculty promotion and tenure decisions, and thus, it is faculty members who must address the issue. In fact, since 1990 there has been widespread campus attention directed toward faculty priorities and rewards. In a review of materials generated by 50 different campus task forces, one researcher concludes that "the master issue is not how hard faculty work but what tasks faculty should work on."[26] That researcher reports that the great majority of faculty, even those at the most prestigious universities, agree that teaching is undervalued. They believe that not only should the status be raised, but also that the roles faculty perform—teaching, research, and service—need to be redefined and made more inclusive of a variety of activities than they have in the past. Despite such broad agreement, real change must be initiated at the department level and there will be resistance to change.[27] The typical department makes decisions by consensus with virtually no leadership because the chair sees himself or herself as temporary, soon to return to faculty responsibilities, and thus, eager to maintain the status quo.[28]

In a provocative discussion of "Faculty Time in the 21st Century," one writer argues that faculty are being challenged to "be accountable, not only for *how* we spend our time, but for the *results* of our time on task in terms of our institution's mission." The writer contends that higher education will be fundamentally restructured in the next decade, and that unless faculty address the concerns of the public, faculty's work will be marginalized, and time-honored traditions such as tenure, academic freedom, and sabbaticals increasingly will be under attack.[29] This writer's own comment will raise the hackles of many a faculty member: "There is nothing inherent in the concept of tenure that says faculty can do what they want, when they want."[30]

Although much of the criticism of faculty priorities is directed at those employed at large public research universities, all faculty cannot help but feel the shift in the public perception of their worth and contribution. At the same time that faculty are coming to realize that they themselves must confront the attack on their profession, they also are resentful of what they see as the lack of effective leadership to enhance their image with their various publics.[31]

Their Perception of Leadership and Governance

A report on the academic profession underscores the lack of confidence faculty have in administrators.[32] Of the U.S. faculty responding to the survey, 45 percent agreed that communication between the faculty and the administration is poor, 58 percent agreed that the administration is often autocratic, and only 39 percent agreed that top-level administrators are providing competent leadership. Researchers speculate that, as faculty have organized into more centralized departments and divisions, they have become increasingly removed from issues affecting the institution as a whole.[33] There is evidence that faculty place the most faith in the strength of the leaders closest to them (i.e., department chairs) and that their confidence lessens as the distance between themselves and their leaders increases (i.e., deans, senior administrators, presidents, board members).[34]

There is nothing new about the adversarial relationship between faculty and senior administrators, but the need for joint effort to meet tough challenges has never been more apparent. As noted earlier, many of the changes needed to address current concerns regarding student outcomes and faculty's priorities are within the purview of the faculty. Senior administrators need to work with existing systems of campus governance to even begin the dialogue that can address these concerns. Unfortunately, faculty have as little faith in the efficacy of their own processes of governance as they do in leadership. Researchers described faculty as dispirited due to their loss of influence over decisions that affect their work and work environment.[35] Similarly, another report indicated that 64 percent of the U.S. faculty respondents felt "not at all influential" in helping to shape key academic policies at the institutional level.[36] Faculty, particularly those at research universities, expect administrators to make decisions within their purview but also expect to have autonomy over the core content of their work.[37]

There is a fundamental dilemma facing administrators and faculty leaders within institutions seeking to realign campus priorities in light of budget shortfalls or public pressure for increased quality in undergraduate education. It is the administration that is charged with dealing with the lack of resources or meeting state mandates for accountability; but to the extent that such decisions affect the academic core, the faculty is required to review plans and be involved. The faculty's role in governance is often criticized "for being too sluggish, too obstructive, and too predisposed to preserving the existing apportionment of jobs and resources."[38] Faculty processes of governance are deliberative and, as a result, time-consuming. At the same time, faculty criticize the administration for adopting increasingly corporate models for decision making that undermine the role of faculty in decisions that have a direct effect on the academic core, such as the worth and viability of specific academic programs.[39] The shared authority that is needed between senior administrators and faculty must be built on trust and cooperation—rare commodities in this strained environment of higher education.[40]

And What about Special Groups of Faculty such as Women, Minorities, and Part-Time Employees?

The literature on the experiences of ethnic and racial minority and women faculty is considerable. Most efforts to examine their experiences relative to their white male peers indicate that they are isolated, lonely, and marginalized.[41] Their distribution continues to be skewed by institutional type, academic rank, and tenure status with ethnic and racial minority and women faculty tending to occupy positions in the least prestigious institutions at the lowest ranks and without tenure.[42]

Women

The most pervasive disparity in women faculty members' experience may be in salary. Salary inequities have been documented across all academic ranks, in virtually every field, and in every type of institution.[43] Disparities also exist in the workload women faculty carry. They spend less time in research-related activities and more time in teaching and in service to the institution.[44] Data indicate that women tend to be promoted and tenured more slowly than male faculty, and they are more likely to leave an institution prior to going up for tenure.[45]

Women report more difficulties in relationships with departmental chairs and colleagues; and they describe themselves as "outsiders," feeling that they do not belong.[46] The majority of women faculty at one public university felt that their work was undervalued because of their gender.[47]

Ethnic and Racial Minority Faculty

The experience of ethnic and racial minority faculty parallels, in many respects, the experiences of women. Although the research on minority group members is limited, there is growing evidence that they experience severe marginalization.[48] They cite everyday interactions, both social and professional, as sources of their feeling unwelcomed, unappreciated, and unwanted. They perceive that colleagues assume they were hired for affirmative action purposes; thus, they feel pressured to continually prove that they deserve their positions.[49]

Minorities face a number of barriers in the tenure review process: they tend to hold more split or joint appointments; they often value teaching and service, which is less likely to be recognized or rewarded, and spend more time on these activities as well as on student advising and they are often isolated and without mentors.[50] Minority faculty perceive more tenure pressure than do their white male peers, and feel their graduate preparation for the faculty role is more of a barrier to their advancement.[51]

Clearly, ethnic and racial minority and women faculty experience academe differently from their white male counterparts. It is evident from the literature that the reality of the faculty experience for these groups is largely negative on many campuses and any institutional assessment of morale needs to take into account gender, ethnicity, and race.

Part-Time Employees

Another group that deserves far more attention than it receives are the numerous faculty members who hold part-time or adjunct positions within colleges and universities. One report indicates that part-time faculty hold 38 percent of the faculty appointments nationally.[52] These faculty are typically underpaid, contracted from semester to semester, and work without benefits.[53] Many hold down full-time loads, semester after semester, at poverty-level wages. As pressures have mounted on instructional budgets, employing part-time faculty has been a cost-saving measure. In these tough times, it will be tempting to cut the positions entirely or to increase the use of part-time or adjunct faculty—either avenue raises troubling questions about the conditions of the work lives of part-time faculty.

As the foregoing descriptions suggest, the issues that these special groups face undoubtedly have an effect on their morale. Moreover, they are not immune to the frustrations of faculty in general. The pressures on faculty are real; they have consequences, not only for individual faculty members, but also for the quality of the academic enterprise. Some would argue that faculty are highly critical by nature and that they will always complain, particularly about administrators and their decisions. It is clear, however, that the majority of faculty care mightily about the quality of teaching and student learning. Faculty vitality is critical to higher education. Faculty deserve to be supported in their efforts to provide the caliber of research, teaching, and service the society needs, and their morale deserves the attention of those who can make a difference—senior administrators.

Notes

1. Finkelstein, M. 1984. *The American Academic Profession: A Synthesis of Social Scientific Inquiry Since World War II*. Columbus: Ohio State University Press, p. 226.

2. *Chronicle of Higher Education Almanac*. (September 1, 1994). The Nation: Faculty and Staff, *41* (1), 31–33.

3. Boyer, E. L. 1990. *Scholarship Reconsidered: Priorities of the Professoriate*. Princeton, New Jersey: Carnegie Foundation for the Advancement of Teaching.

4. Rice, R. E. and A. E. Austin. 1988. "High Faculty Morale: What Exemplary Colleges Do Right." *Change* 20 (2), p. 50–58.

5. Becher, T. 1994. "The Significance of Disciplinary Differences." *Studies in Higher Education* 19 (2), p. 151–61.

6. Biglan, A. 1973. "The Characteristics of Subject Matter in Different Academic Areas." *Journal of Applied Psychology* 57 (2), p. 195–203.

7. Becher, "The Significance of Disciplinary Differences."

8. Becher, T. 1989. *Academic Tribes and Territories: Intellectual Enquiry and the Cultures of Disciplines*. Milton Keynes, United Kingdom: Open University Press.

9. Boyer, E. L., P. G. Altbach, and M. Whitelaw. 1994. *The Academic Profession: An International Perspective*. Princeton, New Jersey: Carnegie Foundation for the Advancement of Teaching.

10. Bowen, H. R. and J. H. Schuster. 1986. *American Professors: A National Resource Imperiled.* Oxford: Oxford University Press.

11. Boyer, Altbach, and Whitelaw, *The Academic Profession.*

12. Hamermesh, D. S. 1994. "Plus Ça Change: The Annual Report on the Economic Status of the Profession, 1993-94." *Academe* 80 (2), p. 5-13.

13. Moore, K. M. and M. J. Amey. 1993. *Making Sense of the Dollars: The Costs and Uses of Faculty Compensation.* ASHE-ERIC Higher Education Report No. 4. Washington DC: The George Washington University, School of Education and Human Development.

14. Bowen and Schuster, *American Professors.*

15. Kerlin, S. P. and D. M. Dunlap. 1993. "For Richer, for Poorer: Faculty Morale in Periods of Austerity and Retrenchment." *Journal of Higher Education* 64 (3), p. 348-77.

16. Grassmuck, K. "Big Increases in Academic-Support Staffs Prompt Growing Concerns on Campuses," *The Chronicle of Higher Education*, 28 Mar. 1990, p. A1, 32-33.

17. Rhoades, G. 1995. "Rising Administrative Costs in Instructional Units." *Thought & Action* 11 (1), p. 7-24.

18. Bok, Derek. 1992. "Reclaiming the Public Trust." *Change* 24 (4), p. 12-19; Edgerton, R. 1993. "The Re-Examination of Faculty Priorities." *Change* 25 (4), p. 10-25; Kennedy, D. 1995. "Another Century's End, Another Revolution for Higher Education." *Change* 27 (3), p. 8-15.

19. Boyer, Altbach, and Whitelaw, *The Academic Profession.*

20. Tack, M. W. and C. L. Patitu. 1992. *Faculty Job Satisfaction: Women and Minorities in Peril.* ASHE-ERIC Higher Education Report No. 4. Washington DC: The George Washington University, School of Education and Human Development.

21. Miller, M. A. 1994. "Pressure to Measure Faculty Work." *Faculty Workload,* 84 (1-3), New Directions for Institutional Research, ed. J. F. Wergin, San Francisco: Jossey-Bass.

22. National Center for Education Statistics. 1991. *Digest of Education Statistics 1991.* Washington DC: U.S. Department of Education, Office of Educational Research and Improvement.

23. Mingle, J. R. 1993. "Faculty Work and Costs/Quality/Access Collision." *AAHE Bulletin* 12 (3), p. 3-6, 12; Wergin, J. F. 1994. "Editor's Notes." In *Analyzing Faculty Workload* 83 (1-3), New Directions for Institutional Research, ed. Wergin, J. F. San Francisco: Jossey-Bass; Dey, E. L. 1995. "The Activities of Undergraduate Teaching Faculty." *Thought and Action* 11 (1), p. 43-62.

24. Dey, "The Activities of Undergraduate Teaching Faculty."

25. Boyer, *Scholarship Reconsidered.*

26. Edgerton, "The Re-Examination of Faculty Priorities," p. 14.

27. Edgerton, "The Re-Examination of Faculty Priorities."

28. Kennedy, "Another Century's End."

29. Plater, W. M. 1995. "Future Work: Faculty Time in the 21st Century." *Change* 27 (3), p. 22-33.

30. Plater "Future Work," p. 32.

31. Currie, J. November 1994. "The Changing Nature of Academic Work: Case Study of Florida State University."

32. Boyer, Altbach, and Whitelaw, *The Academic Profession*.

33. Boyer, Altbach, and Whitelaw, *The Academic Profession*.

34. Johnsrud, L. K. 1994. *University of Hawaii-Manoa Faculty Morale Study*. Honolulu: University of Hawaii at Manoa, Faculty Senate.

35. Bowen and Schuster, *American Professors*.

36. Boyer, Altbach, and Whitelaw, *The Academic Profession*.

37. Copur, H. 1990. "Academic Professionals: A Study of Conflict and Satisfaction in the Professoriate." *Human Relations* 43 (2), p. 113–127.

38. Schuster, J. H., D. G. Smith, K. A. Corak, and M. M. Yamada. 1994. *Strategic Governance: How to Make Big Decisions Better*. Phoenix, Arizona: American Council on Education/Oryx Press.

39. Gumport, P. J. 1993. "The Contested Terrain of Academic Program Reduction." *Journal of Higher Education* 64 (3), p. 283–311.

40. Mortimer, K. P. and T. R. McConnell. 1978. *Sharing Authority Effectively*. San Francisco: Jossey-Bass.

41. Johnsrud, L. K. 1993. "Women and Minority Faculty Experience: Responding to Diverse Realities." In *Supporting a Diverse Faculty*, ed. Gainen J. and R. Boice. San Francisco: Jossey-Bass, p. 3–16.

42. Russell, S. H.1991. "The Status of Women and Minorities in Higher Education: Findings from the 1988 National Survey of Postsecondary Findings." *CUPA Journal* 42 (1), p. 1–11.

43. Moore and Amey, *Making Sense of Dollars*.

44. Armour, R., B. Fuhrmann, and J. F. Wergin. 1990. "Racial and Gender Difference in Faculty Careers." Paper presented at the meeting of the American Educational Research Association, Boston, MA; Finkelstein, *The American Academic Professor*; Davis, D. E. and H. S. Astin. 1990. "Life Cycle, Career Pattern and Gender Stratification in Academe: Breaking Myths and Exposing Truths." In *Storming the Tower: Women in the Academic World*, ed. Lie, S. and V. E. O'Leary. London: Kogan & Page; Russell, "The Status of Women and Minorities in Higher Education"; Carnegie Foundation for the Advancement of Teaching. 1990. "Women Faculty Excel as Campus Citizens." *Change* 22 (5), p. 39–43.

45. Finkelstein, *The American Academic Professor*; Johnsrud, L. K. and C. D. Des Jarlais. 1994. "Barriers to the Retention and Tenure of Women and Minorities: The Case of a University's Faculty." *Review of Higher Education* 17 (4), p. 335–53; Rausch, D. K., B. P. Ortiz, R. A. Douthill, and L. L. Reed. 1989. "The Academic Revolving Door: Why Do Women Get Caught?" *CUPA Journal* 40 (1), p. 1–16.

46. Johnsrud and Des Jarlais, "Barriers to the Retention and Tenure of Men and Minorities"; Aisenberg, N. and M. Harrington. 1988. *Women of Academe: Outsiders in the Sacred Grove*. Amherst: University of Massachusetts Press.

47. Parsons, L. A., R. G. Sands, and J. Duane. 1991. "The Campus Climate for Women Faculty at a Public University." *Initiatives* 54 (1), p. 19–27.

48. Aguirre, A., Jr., R. Martinez, and A. Hernandez. 1993. "Majority and Minority Faculty Perceptions in Academe." *Research in Higher Education* 34 (3), p. 371–85; Boice, R. 1993. "Early Turning Points in Professional Careers of Women and Minorities." In *Supporting a Diverse Faculty*, ed. Gainen, J. and R. Boice. San Francisco: Jossey-Bass, p. 71–79; Johnsrud, L. K. and K. C. Sadao. 1993. "Ethnic and Racial Minority Faculty within a Research University: Their Common Experiences." Paper presented at the annual meeting of the Association for the Study of Higher Education, Pittsburgh, PA.

49. Menges R. J. and W. H. Exum. 1983. "Barriers to the Progress of Women and Minority Faculty." *Journal of Higher Education* 54 (2), p. 123–43; Luz Reyes, M. L. and J. J. Halcon. 1988. "Racism in Academia: The Old Wolf Revisited." *Harvard Educational Review* 58 (2), p. 229–314.

50. Menges and Exum, "Barriers to the Progress of Women and Minority Faculty"; Banks, W. M. 1984. "Afro-American Scholars in the University: Roles and Conflicts." *American Behavioral Scientist* 27, p. 325–39; McEvans, A. E. and D. Appelbaum. 1992. "Minority Faculty in Research Universities: Barriers to Progress." Paper presented at the American Educational Research Association, San Francisco, CA; Boice, "Early Turning Points."

51. Johnsrud and Des Jarlais, "Barriers to the Retention and Tenure of Women and Minorities."

52. American Association of University Professors. 1993. "The Status of Non-Tenured Track Faculty." *Academe* 79 (4), p. 39–46.

53. Unger, Donald N. S. 1995. "Academic Apartheid: The Predicament of Part-time Faculty." *Thought & Action* 9 (1), p. 117–20.

Chapter 6

Assessing Morale

It is not nearly so important who initiates a morale assessment as who is involved in the process. The effort can come from the top (the president's office or other executive-level administrators), the middle (the human resource/personnel office or a council of deans or directors), or the grassroots (the administrative staff and faculty themselves). To simplify this discussion, assume that the effort is initiated by a human resource office and that it has the blessing and support of the president or appropriate vice president. Needless to say, whatever top-level support is garnered up front will further the chances that the effort will make a difference in the end. This chapter describes the steps necessary to launch a successful assessment, from project leadership, to the assessment design, to analysis of data.

Project Leadership

To ensure the success of the project, three leadership issues must be addressed: Who will convene the project and serve as spokesperson? Who will do the actual assessment? Who will provide ongoing advice and represent diverse interests? Ideally, the project requires a chairperson, a principal investigator, and an advisory board. Decisions about the principal investigator and an advisory board may precede the selection of a chair for the project. Human resource personnel may serve to convene the first meeting of the advisory group; the convenor of the group can serve as chair or the group can elect a chair depending on the norms of the campus.

The Principal Investigator

Deciding on the person who will conduct the assessment is a critical issue. Two primary considerations are (1) the expertise to do the work, and (2) the trust and respect of all concerned parties. The type of assessment advocated in this guide involves both qualitative and quantitative approaches. Thus, whoever conducts the assessment needs to be competent with both approaches or there needs to be a team of investigators with complementary skills to work on the project. On some campuses, there is a deep chasm between qualitative and quantitative researchers. If it is decided to go with a team of researchers, it is exceedingly important to identify those who are able and willing to work together.

The trust and respect afforded the principal investigator depends first on the confidentiality of raw data and second on the unbiased interpretation of the results. Every effort must be taken to ensure that responses are entirely confidential. Anonymity and confidentiality are different. Anonymity indicates that the responses *cannot* be associated with individuals; confidentiality indicates that the responses *will not* be associated with individuals. Often it is clear to participants that their responses are not anonymous because of the demographic information that is requested or the coding (if it is used). The principal investigator must be perceived to be a neutral party or with no personal interest in individual responses. All those involved must ensure that interest is in patterns only, that no response will ever be associated with an individual respondent, and that confidentiality is absolutely guaranteed. This guarantee must be reiterated with conviction; also it is essential that it be honored without exception.

The second concern is with interpretation. If morale is low and distrust high on the campus, the credibility of the assessment must be ensured. If the assessment effort appears to be coopted by any single department, those affected will suspect that their real concerns will be ignored and an inaccurate picture presented. The principal investigator should be well-known and highly respected. It should be made clear that the principal investigator will work closely with the advisory board, which also will serve as a check on the interpretation.

Who is most likely to have both the expertise and the trustworthiness? The best choice for principal investigator is going to differ by campus. At some institutions, members of institutional research would be the obvious choice; at others, they are seen as an arm of the senior administration and would not be trusted. On some campuses, individual faculty who do research, using survey instruments and/or interview techniques, may be the best choice. Faculty from departments such as educational leadership, higher education, sociology of work, or human resource management may have the interest and expertise to conduct the assessment. On other campuses, it may be best to get outside expertise (e.g., consultants who specialize in higher education human resource issues). This last option may be the least likely given the limited discretionary resources available on many campuses today. In fact, the issue of resources for the project is a delicate one.

Advisory Board

The best way to alleviate misunderstandings and suspicions about a large-scale assessment effort is to gather a representative group that will serve as advisers to the project. Selecting appropriate individuals to participate on the Board serves several purposes: it signals the openness of the process, it garners the trust and support of those with a stake in the outcome, it draws those into the process who might otherwise ignore the effort, and it ensures that there will be a group committed to dissemination of results and action.

If the morale of both the administrative staff and faculty are to be assessed, it may be best to have two advisory boards or two working groups within one board, or to conduct one assessment at a time. Two groups may be needed because the necessary representation differs and the issues differ sufficiently for the two groups so that two assessment tools may be needed. The amount of work required for such a large-scale assessment also may be too much for one group to accomplish in a timely manner.

The appropriate makeup of either board is dependent on the politics of the particular campus. The goal is to gather a group of individuals together that will be committed to the project and whose representation will give the assessment credibility. The group could easily number between 10 and 15 people. The representatives on a board to conduct an administrative staff assessment might include: a human resources officer, a vice president of administration, a union representative, an institutional researcher, administrative staff representatives from each administrative unit (e.g., academic affairs, student affairs, business affairs, and external affairs) or from each functional grouping (e.g., technicians, professionals, directors, coordinators, etc.), and representatives of special interest groups (e.g., commissions on the status of women or ethnic and racial minority groups or other advocacy groups).

The representatives on a board to conduct a faculty assessment might include: a human resources officer, a vice president of academic affairs, a faculty senate representative, a union representative, an institutional researcher, faculty representatives from either academic groupings (e.g., humanities, social sciences, natural sciences and the professions) or from categories of faculty (e.g., instructional faculty, researchers, librarians, extension agents, specialists), and representatives of special interest groups (e.g., commissions on the status of women or ethnic and racial minority groups or other advocacy groups).

The drawback of any advisory board is that it can be cantankerous and it often has more advice than the convenor or the principal investigator appreciates. On the other hand, its advice is often good and it can help avoid the pitfalls that those working in isolation cannot anticipate.

There are a number of tasks that need to be accomplished either at or prior to the first meeting of the board. The board can be used to react to possible choices for the principal investigator or, if the decision has been made, the principal investigator should attend the initial meeting to discuss the procedures of the assessment and specifically how the board will be involved. Two other matters must be clarified for the members of the advisory board:

Purpose of Assessment

Assuming the purpose of the assessment has been established, it needs to be articulated. For example: "We are concerned about the morale of X group's members, and we are conducting an assessment to determine those factors that have an effect on their morale, either positive or negative. The purpose of the assessment is to make recommendations to the senior administration or appropriate individuals that will help improve the morale of X group's members." It is important the purpose is clearly stated and understood by members of the advisory board. Also, the purpose will have to be included in any news release as well as cover letters that are sent to encourage members of the administrative staff or faculty to participate.

Resources for the Assessment

If there are insufficient resources to conduct the project, that fact will be a source of criticism and will reinforce the notion that the senior administration does not care about the morale of the staff. If too much is spent on the project, it will be perceived as untimely, frivolous, or ill-advised. Obviously, the costs must be kept as low as possible.

The major expenses are the principal investigator's time, the data entry and/or transcription services, duplicating fees, and cost of envelopes. There are creative means to handle the principal investigator's time, particularly if it involves faculty. Release time, access to data after the project is completed, and graduate assistants are all of value to faculty. Although those are costs, they are often already in the budget and at least do not represent new monies. If clerical support and supplies can be covered by the human resource office, the costs can be kept to a minimum. Further, the primary purpose of this book is to provide a guide as well as sample instruments that will save individual campuses time and money. Nonetheless, such an effort will require dedicated board members willing to volunteer their time and energy.

Designing the Assessment

The actual design of the assessment for a particular campus needs to be determined by the principal investigator in conjunction with members of the advisory board. The following recommendations describe an assessment that has been conducted at one large public university and is doable. The assessment design also combines both qualitative and quantitative data gathering. All the documents are included in the appendix and are referred to as appropriate.

Review of the Literature

The first step in the process should be a review of the existing literature on the quality of work life of the administrative staff and faculty. There is no point in starting from scratch; on the other hand, the scholarly background and interests of the principal investigator may determine the extent of this review. The previous two chapters (Chapters 4 and 5) of this book provide summary reviews of the literature and the factors that others have established as important to quality of work life of administrative staff and faculty, respectively.

Human Subjects Review

Although the approval of the human subjects review board/committee cannot be sought until the design is determined, it is included here as a precaution. Campus regulations differ, but it is essential that they be followed. Keeping the protection of human subjects foremost in mind while designing the method of assessment is the best way to ensure the participants will be protected from harm.

The Qualitative Assessment

The purpose of the qualitative assessment is primarily to facilitate the creation of a quantitatively based survey instrument that reflects the concerns unique to the campus. The steps necessary to generate a comprehensive survey instrument include: a review of the existing literature; gathering qualitative data via individual interviews or focus groups; analyzing the qualitative data to identify items to be included on a survey; and finally, drafting an instrument to be reviewed by the board. Ultimately, this qualitative effort will identify factors that will be incorporated into an instrument that can be mailed to every individual member of the administrative staff or faculty. The survey instrument will ensure representation for every individual; the qualitative method is designed to ensure the instrument is as thorough and inclusive as possible, given the restraints of time and cost.

Qualitative methods generate data that are rich and full of the anecdotal experiences of the participants. These data reveal particular issues that may not surface in the review of the literature or may not occur to the advisory board or the principal investigator. The two primary methods for data gathering are individual interviews or focus groups. Focus groups potentially provide an opportunity for anyone who chooses to participate, while interviews are necessarily more selective due to the time involved. The choice may depend on the time and resources available. Using both methods also is a possibility. The following discussion provides practical tips on how to use interviews or focus groups for data gathering. For a more complete guide to these qualitative methods, several resources are listed at the end of this chapter.

Individual Interviews

Individuals can be selected in a variety of ways; whatever means is chosen should be systematic and determined in consultation with the advisory board. One possibility is to choose key informants who are selected on criteria such as their leadership positions, the respect of their peers, or their candor. It also is important to consider their representativeness across work unit, age, rank, gender, race, or any other criteria that may uncover factors that influence their quality of work life. The difficulty of conducting enough interviews to be representative is substantial.

A semistructured interview protocol should be designed based on factors identified in the literature concerning quality of work life on other campuses as well as the recommendations of the advisory board. The interview protocol should be designed to encourage an informant directed interview session. Questions need to be structured to avoid leading the informant. For example, presenting general questions first such as: "What has your administrative/faculty experience been like here at the university?" and "Do you face any challenges working here?" allows flexibility in responding.

Appendix 1 includes a sample letter on page 131 inviting faculty members to participate in interviews. This letter can be easily adapted for use with administrators. Confidentiality needs to be emphasized as well as the purpose of the interviews. If the interviews are taped (with the written or taped consent of the interviewee), a transcript can be generated that is complete and accurate. It is possible, also, for a skilled interviewer to simply listen for factors that need to be included in further assessments. The latter approach is less labor intensive (transcription time is eliminated) but, again, it is best if the decision is made by the advisory board.

Focus Groups

Focus groups also can be used to gather data for the survey instrument. The purpose of focus groups is to probe individual experiences for in-depth information in a group setting. Because focus groups provide for interaction on a topic rather than singular responses, participants tend to bounce ideas off one another and build on what others have said. Members of the advisory board can serve as convenors of the groups if they are comfortable doing so; otherwise, respected campus leaders of the particular group (either administrative staff or faculty) should be asked to lead the discussion. These individuals should be skilled facilitators to keep the group focused on the topic of concern—the quality of work life; the leaders should ensure no individual or small group of individuals dominate the discussion and that everyone gets the opportunity to speak. A recorder is needed to record the specifics of the discussion. Group members should be assured that their names will not be used; nonetheless, confidentiality is dependent on the honor of the group. Groups should probably be composed of 8 to 10 individuals from similar work units.

The number of focus groups should be determined by the advisory board. One campus effort, which focused on faculty, structured its groups similar to New England town meetings and scheduled faculty to meet in their disciplinary areas. Thus, all members of the faculty were invited to participate and nearly 300 did so.[1] This sort of large-scale effort generates *huge* amounts of data and has the advantage of involving large numbers of individuals in a process that can be morale enhancing in and of itself. On the other hand, if the intent is more narrowly defined to generate factors that will then be included on a survey to which all can respond, the number of groups can be greatly reduced.

Appendix 1 (on page 132) includes a sample letter of invitation (directed to administrative staff) to participate in a focus group. The rule seems to be to invite widely and expect less than half to show. Be prepared with extra facilitators and recorders in case the response is larger at any one time. For further discussion of the use of focus groups, see the resources at the end of the chapter.

Analysis of the Qualitative Data

If extensive interviews and/or focus group data are generated, then the qualitative analysis can become a stand-alone report. It should be analyzed by a qualitative methodologist who is adept at identifying themes and patterns in the data and who will create a document that reflects and honors the tone and content of the response.

If the intent of the interviews and/or focus groups were limited to generating factors to be included in a survey instrument, the analysis can be more limited in scope. Lists should be created that name factors in the language used by the respondents. For example, year-end evaluation may be performance review to one group, colleague/peer review to another, and contract renewal to yet another. These factors, then, become items on the quantitatively based survey instrument list.

Quantitative Assessment

There are countless models that can be followed to create a survey instrument. Two samples are included: Appendix 2 on page 139 contains a sample to be used with administrative staff, and Appendix 3 on page 144 includes a sample to be used with faculty. These samples are revised versions of instruments actually used at the University of Hawaii. The original versions also appear in the case study technical reports in Chapters 8 and 9. Both were created from some combination of literature review, interviews, focus groups, pilot tests, and feedback from advisory groups. The sample instruments provide a place to begin, and can easily be modified to include items specific to a particular campus. Brief explanations of the quantitative assessment instruments' sections follow.

Introduction

The purpose of the survey instrument and the definition of morale should be made clear; the scaling should be clarified. In these examples, different versions of Likert scales are used. The meaning of the extremes should be emphasized and the midpoint explained. The "not applicable" option may be included so respondents are not confused by what does not apply to them personally.

Item or Factor Scaling

This section provides the essential information about which factors have a negative effect on the respondents and which have a positive effect. The items included should be narrowly focused (i.e., not overlapping, not "ethnic *and* gender diversity of work unit"); clear (e.g., one sample item, "autonomy," was dropped for lack of clarity); and comprehensive (include "other" so respondents can write in what has been missed). Clustering the items into categories helps the respondents focus on one area at a time and breaks up the lists to maintain the respondents' interest.

It is important to clarify that respondents are to rate the item based on their *current* work situation, the item's effect on their *personal* level of morale, and to think in terms of *what is*, not how they would feel *if* the item or their situation were somehow different. These cautions are based on questions respondents asked. Instruction clarification will reduce response error as well as save the respondents time and frustration.

Note that the two instruments differ in approach. The administrative survey (Appendix 2) seeks responses relating both to effect (negative or positive) and to importance. The faculty survey (Appendix 3) asks only for degree of effect. The administrator version is longer but ensures that both intensity and direction of effect are measured.

Item or Factor Ranking

Asking respondents to rank, in order of importance, the items they have just scaled forces them to think differently about the items. Numerous items may have be ranked very important, but now respondents must indicate which of those items are most important. Also, analysis of this section yields a cumulative percentage of the issues that most respondents consider important. If both intensity (importance) and direction (negative or positive) are measured on each item, this ranking may be redundant and can be omitted.

Overall Morale

Individuals respond to three types of statements to provide an overall reading of their morale: (1) statements regarding their feelings about their job, (2) statements regarding their feelings about their institution, and (3) a specific statement about the level of their morale. Together, the responses to these statements generate a "morale score," which can be used to compare groups or as a dependent variable (i.e., the analysis can determine which of the items or factors listed predict overall morale).

Demographic Information

The demographic information requested has two purposes: (1) to describe the representativeness of the respondents and (2) to partition the data by relevant categories to test for significant differences. In other words, this information allows an analysis of differences by categories such as years of experience, job classification, school or work unit, gender, age, and ethnicity and race. Certainly there are other kinds of information that can be requested but the length of the instrument is always a concern.

Pilot Testing the Instrument

Once the instrument is drafted, it should be pilot tested with the advisory board as well as a small group of potential respondents. Items or statements that are not clear should be clarified or omitted. The assessment instrument should be analyzed to be sure it is collecting the appropriate data in the form needed. This step is exceedingly important, and one that is too often omitted in survey research. Once the survey is distributed, it is too late to adjust for mistakes or misunderstandings.

Analysis of the Quantitative Data

Obviously, the analysis will vary depending on the form of the instrument designed. The following general suggestions are made in regard to the recommended versions in Appendixes 2 and 3.

Demographic Data

The characteristics of the respondents should be described in frequencies and percentages. Include distribution of response by demographics such as gender, race, age, and classification to give a sense of how representative the response is. If demographic information is available on the population, that can be presented also. Anomalies should be noted.

Descriptive Data

Means and standard deviations can be provided on each survey item. Knowing the number who responded to each item also is helpful in understanding the results. The highest and lowest means are of interest and should be highlighted in the discussion. If both intensity (importance) and direction (negative or positive) are measured, a "gap" score can be presented (i.e., the difference between the importance and the direction on any given item).

Item or Factor Ranking

Analysis of the item ranking yields a cumulative percentage of the issues that most respondents consider to be most important (both positive and negative). The cumulative percentage represents the total percentage of the first, second, and third choices of any item.

Composite Scales and Comparative Data

Scales can be calculated for aggregated indicators of each substantive area. For example, two scales have been created for the sample administrative staff results: one for institutional factors and one for professional factors. The sample faculty results have nine groups of items that are aggregated into scales. The composite scores are stronger indicators because they are compiled from individual items plus they reduce the number of indicators for comparative purposes. In other words, rather than trying to determine whether there are significant gender differences on individual items (which can number from 70 to 80), the composites can be used. Tests for significant differences (t-tests or analysis of variance as appropriate) should be conducted on all the variables of interest (e.g., gender, race, age, and classification) and the composite scales.

Overall Morale

The two sample surveys provide different means to examine overall morale. On the faculty survey, the question was asked about change in morale because there existed earlier data that could be compared. A simple mean was calculated. On both surveys, there are several questions that can be aggregated to

determine an overall morale score. The overall score can be reported and compared for the various groups of interest. This score also can be used as a dependent variable in a regression model to determine which factors or scales predict
morale.

After the instrument is in final form another set of issues arise, such as who
should receive the instrument, who approves the content of the cover letter,
and what type of coding and follow-up should be used. Those issues are addressed in Chapter 7.

Notes

1.   Lincoln,Y. S., C. Marshall, and A. E. Austin, "Institutionally-Based Quality
     of Worklife Assessment: The Politics of 'Do It Yourself.'" Paper presented
     at the annual meeting of the American Educational Research Association,
     San Francisco, CA, April 1992).

Resources for Designing the Assessment

Focus Groups

Morgan, D. L. 1988. *Focus Groups As Qualitative Research*. Newbury Park,
     CA: Sage Publications.
Shaffir, W. B. and R. A. Stebbins. 1991. *Experiencing Fieldwork: An Inside
     View of Qualitative Research*. Newbury Park, CA: Sage Publications.
Sherman, R. R. and R. B. Webb. 1988. *Qualitative Research in Education:
     Focus and Methods*. New York: Falmer Press.

Interviewing

Marshall, C. and G. B. Rossman. 1989. *Designing Qualitative Research*.
     Newbury Park, CA: Sage Publications.
McCracken, G. D. 1988. *The Long Interview*. Beverly Hills, CA: Sage
     Publications.
Robson, S. and A. Foster. 1989. *Qualitative Research in Action*. London: E.
     Arnold.
Seidman, I. E. 1991. *Interviewing as Qualitative Research: A Guide for
     Researchers in Education and the Social Sciences*. New York: Teachers
     College Press.
Weller, S. C. and A. K. Romney. 1988. *Systematic Data Collection*. Newbury
     Park, CA: Sage Publications.

Survey Design and Analysis

Alwin, D. F. 1978. *Survey Design and Analysis: Current Issues*. Beverly Hills,
     CA: Sage Publications.
Burgess, R. and A. Bryman. 1994. *Analyzing Qualitative Data*. New York:
     Routledge.

Conner, R. F. 1981. *Methodological Advances in Evaluation Research*. Beverly Hills, CA: Sage Publications; Published in cooperation with the Evaluation Research Society.

Dillman, D. A. 1978. *Mail and Telephone Surveys: The Total Design Method*. New York: John Wiley & Sons.

Miller, D. C. 1991. *Handbook of Research Design and Social Measurement*. Newbury Park, CA: Sage Publications, 5th edition.

Chapter 7

Issues of Assessment

Once the survey instrument is in final form and ready for mailing, a number of other issues arise that require decisions by the principal investigator with the advice of the advisory board. These issues require judgment calls. There are no simple right or wrong answers, but it is important informed decisions are made and that the rationale for those decisions can be communicated to those who express concern during the project.

Sample or Population to Be Surveyed

Deciding who should receive and respond to the survey instrument is important. Most large-scale surveys use a sampling design to save time and money. A well-conceived system for drawing a random stratified sample ensures that results will be representative of the population from which the sample is drawn. For research purposes, a random sample is perfectly acceptable; in fact, some would argue that drawing a sample is preferable to a census-style population approach. When an entire population is surveyed, there is simply more of everything to handle (instruments, envelopes, addresses, code numbers, follow-up letters, complaints, and ultimately, more data to enter and analyze) and the likelihood of nonsampling errors increases.

On the other hand, the purpose of the survey is to assess morale and one point that has been made repeatedly is that the process itself is intended to enhance morale. It may well be counterproductive for one administrative staff or faculty member to receive a copy of the survey while a colleague next door does not have the opportunity to respond because he or she happened not to be included in the sample. For this reason, the entire population should be surveyed. This decision means that even greater efforts must be made to achieve as high a response rate as possible.

Once the decision has been made to survey the entire population, secure up-to-date lists of all members of the group. Human resource offices are typically the best source but rosters also are kept by groups such as senates and unions. Campus addresses will eliminate mailing costs. Request a master list in alphabetical order as well as three sets of mailing labels.

Cover Letters and Follow-Up

Sample cover letters (one for administrative staff on page 133 and one for faculty on page 134) are included in Appendix 1 and the content is straightforward. The purpose of the morale assessment should be stated and sponsorship of the project should be clarified. Confidentiality should be emphasized. If coding is used, it is important to explain that the coding is meant to facilitate the follow-up and will not be used to identify individual responses. It is always best to give respondents a deadline for follow-up or at least an indication of when a response is expected (e.g., one week from receipt of the survey).

An issue for the advisory board to discuss is from whom the cover letter should come. The role of the cover letter is to increase the response rate; the person who signs it may make a difference. A number of individuals could sign the letter (e.g., a senior administrator for academic or administrative affairs as the sponsor, a human resource official as the initiator, and the chair of the advisory board) but the advisory board should have a frank discussion of the advantages or disadvantages of each of the possibilities. Questions to be considered: Who is known to the respondents? Who is respected and trusted? Who will inspire participation and credibility?

One way to diffuse the effect of the source of the letter is to create letterhead that includes the names of the advisory board members. A well chosen and representative board will allay concerns about any single sponsor of the project and give the board recognition at the same time.

The best response rate will be achieved through a series of mailings. Three mailings are recommended: (1) the survey instrument plus the cover letter; (2) a reminder postcard or letter; and (3) a duplicate of the survey and another letter further encouraging participation. The reminder letter and the second cover letter should be worded to cajole the administrative staff or faculty members to respond. Appendix 1 includes sample follow-up letters on pages 135–138. It is the case that those who respond later often differ in their responses from those who respond immediately; the results of the survey are less likely to be biased if there are multiple mailings and a real effort to enhance the return rate. The response rate may increase from 25 percent on a first mailing to 40 percent on a second to 55 to 70 percent on the final mailing. (See also "Total Design Method," included in the resources listed at the end of Chapter 6, on this issue.)

Coding

Whether to numerically code the instruments for identification is debatable. Placing an identifying code number on the back of each survey instrument (or on the return envelope) eliminates the need to send follow-up requests to those who have already responded. On receipt of the completed survey, the code number is checked and the individual's name is eliminated from future correspondence. The advantage is less cost and less irritation for those who have already responded. The disadvantage is the concern expressed by some respondents that the code number indicates that their response is not anonymous and that confidentiality may be jeopardized.

The principal investigator must be able to ensure confidentiality. A process should be set up in which the raw data are protected. When a survey is returned and the code number checked, a new number should be placed on the front of the instrument that is then used to enter the data. The original code number associated with the individual name is no longer needed. The mailing list of names and code numbers should not be stored with the returned surveys. There is no reason for an individual name to ever be associated with a returned survey.

The third and final mailing, which includes the duplicate survey instrument, does not need to have a code number. The fact that the last mailing is not coded may enhance the final return rate.

It is sometimes argued that if the instruments are coded, then the demographic information should be picked up separately—from institutional records—and not be requested on the survey. The problem with this approach is that it is more likely to compromise individual respondents because it is clear that their names have been associated with their instrument to connect the demographic data. It is recommended to ask respondents to provide demographic data; they then have the option of cutting off the number and/or skipping the demographic section if they so choose.

Analysis of Data and Dissemination of Findings

Once the instruments have been received, the data must be coded, then entered into a statistical software program. The sample survey instruments provided here can be used as they are or they can be adapted to machine-readable format. A machine-readable format eliminates the cost for data entry and decreases human data entry errors. The machine-readable format does demand, however, that the questions conform to the space available. The decision on format will depend on the availability and cost of computer time, as opposed to the availability and cost of data entry, and other factors unique to the campus and the available resources.

The analyses can be simple and straightforward and should be as user-friendly as possible. A summary of findings should be prepared for review by the advisory board prior to dissemination. Chapters 8 and 9 provide case studies of actual morale assessments conducted on administrative staff and faculty, respectively. Samples of the summary of findings including the tables are included. This review serves as a check on the interpretation, tone, and presentation of the findings. It is in no way meant to be disparaging to the principal investigator; the integrity of the findings should not be compromised. The purpose of a review is not to massage, bury, or obfuscate the data. Rather, the summary should be reviewed to ensure the results are presented in the most clear, forthright, and accurate manner as possible.

The dissemination of the results should be as wide as possible. Ideally, if the population was surveyed, the population would receive the results. If the cost is prohibitive, an executive summary should be available to individuals with the option that they can request copies of the full report. Other dissemination options include staff or faculty newsletters, campus newspapers, or presentations at open forums. It is most important to disseminate the results—there should be no sense that the results were "buried." The actual dissemination of the case studies presented here is described in Chapter 10.

Limitations of Method

There are people who simply have no faith in survey data or who think all statistics lie—there is probably no convincing them that the effort has any credibility. On the other hand, there are limitations of the method that should be acknowledged. The quality of the results is entirely dependent on the clarity, relevance, and thoroughness of the instrument, which is why such pains should be taken to identify items and pilot test them for respondent understanding. Another limitation is, of course, the fact that the data are "perceptual"; that is, the data reflect the feelings, attitudes, and beliefs of the respondents. Some critics will dismiss the data as "soft" and prefer more "concrete" measures such as salary differentials or workload indicators. Such measures are certainly relevant to morale, but alone they would not indicate the effect these measures have on individual or group morale. To measure morale, the survey must ask people how they feel, and then do the best job possible to measure those feelings.

Finally, the accuracy of the results are limited by the honesty of respondents. Those who use the survey instrument to blast the institution by simply indicating that "everything is awful" or who respond to "give them what they want to hear" undermine the results. Every effort must be taken to assure respondents that the morale assessment is a genuine effort to identify issues of concern to staff members. Emphasize that the findings not only will be taken seriously, but also will be used to improve the quality of their work life. Perhaps most important, confidentiality must be guaranteed. For respondents to be open and honest about their perceptions, they must trust that their responses are confidential. Respondents who fear reprisal will not be candid in their responses. At the same time, a lack of trust may be one of the main deterrents to high morale on a campus and should not stop the assessment project. The project, with the careful selection of an advisory board and principal investigator, can rise above a climate of paranoia and distrust and provide a valuable service to the campus.

The Politics of Assessment

A morale assessment project can generate a good deal of tension and wariness on the part of members of the campus community. Senior administrators may perceive the project as an effort to make them "look bad" or even as "insubordinate insurrection"; union officials may see the project as an effort to make them "look bad" or to undermine their contract negotiations; some members of the administrative staff and faculty will see the project as waste of time and money or as a sop;

and others will believe that the project is a ploy to identify and punish those who complain about the status quo. If these attitudes are prevalent on a campus, there is a real need for an effort to assess and enhance morale. Nonetheless, these political concerns must be anticipated and/or dealt with as they arise.

To diffuse the distrust, include trusted representatives from each group that has a stake in the project on the advisory board. The chairperson and the principal investigator must keep the board involved and informed so it is able to answer any questions or concerns that arise. The more people who are knowledgeable about the project, the less harm will be done by misinformation and rumor. The leadership of administrative staff or faculty groups needs to be kept informed so it in turn can report the progress of the assessment to constituents. Every effort should be made to complete the project in a timely manner. For example, a year should not pass between data collection and the dissemination of results.

The more negative the climate on the campus is, the greater the need for systematic attention to morale. Unfortunately the more negative the climate, the more difficult it is to conduct an assessment that avoids politics and generates findings that are considered credible. The most positive effect of a morale assessment will come from an assessment that is taken seriously and serves to make a real difference in the quality of work life experienced by administrative staff and faculty.

Chapter 8

Case Study #1:

An Example of a 10-Campus Midlevel Administrator Morale Assessment

The case study presented in this chapter is authentic. This particular assessment was initiated by a graduate student, Vicki J. Rosser, who was interested in studying the working conditions of midlevel administrators. The project grew from a campus-based study to one assessing the morale of midlevel administrators on the 10 campuses of the University of Hawaii System. This chapter describes the process used in conducting the assessment as well as presents the actual findings. The technical report that was generated from data is included.

Data Source

The University of Hawaii System is composed of 10 campuses located on four islands. The 10 campuses include a major research university, a comprehensive four-year institution, a two-year baccalaureate-granting institution, and seven community colleges. The chancellor of the University of Hawaii at Manoa, the research university, also serves as president of the system. The campuses work together as a system in terms of the articulation of students, but they compete with one another for scarce resources.

As a public, state-supported university, all employees are state employees. The administrative group included in this study were all members of the administrative, professional and technical staff, or APTs. This group excludes executive officers such as the president, vice presidents, deans, directors, and other managerial positions for which academic rank or tenure are required.

Instrument Design

To devise a relevant and comprehensive survey instrument, items were generated from a thorough literature review and a series of on-campus interviews. Interviews were conducted with six administrators from one rural community college and three from one four-year research university. The group included individuals working in instruction, administrative services, and community and institutional affairs.

A description of the actual survey instrument is included in the technical report. The original survey instrument also is included at the end of the technical report. As noted earlier, a revised version of the instrument—the one that would be used if the assessment were conducted again—is included in Appendix 2. The primary change from the original is the differentiation between how positive or negative an issue is, and how important it is—a distinction that was less clear in the original. This change also allows a "gap" score to be calculated as described in Chapter 6 in the section on analyzing the data.

Procedures

The survey was mailed to the total population of 1,293 midlevel administrators employed throughout the university system. A series of three mailings was completed over a three-month period. (Samples of the letters are included in Appendix 1 on pages 133, 135 and 136.) The initial mailing included a cover letter indicating support of the project from the Director of Equal Opportunity and Affirmative Action and the System Director of Human Resources. Coding was used on the initial mailing to enhance the return rate; however, individual names were never associated with individual responses, and confidentiality was assured. The second mailing was a reminder notice sent to those who had not responded three weeks after the initial mailing. The third mailing, mailed 10 days after the second, included another reminder and another copy of the instrument. Because a number of potential respondents indicated uneasiness about the anonymity of their responses, the coding was omitted from the last mailing. This process yielded a 70 percent response rate.

Findings of the Survey

The data were analyzed and a technical report was written for dissemination. The technical report is included in its entirety on the following pages.

The University of Hawaii's System

Administrative, Professional, and Technical (APTs)

Staff

Morale Study

Dr. Linda K. Johnsrud, Associate Professor

Vicki J. Rosser, Graduate Research Assistant

Department of Educational Administration

The authors of this report would like to acknowledge the support of
Mie Watanabe, Director of Equal Opportunity and Affirmative Action, and
Peggy Hong, System Director of Human Resources.
The content of the report is, however, the responsibility of the authors.

We also extend our thanks to the hundreds of APTs who responded to the survey.

Spring 1995

The University of Hawai'i System

Administrative, Professional, and Technical (APTs) Staff

Morale Study

EXECUTIVE SUMMARY

A morale survey was distributed to the members of the Administrative, Professional, and Technical (APTs) staff in the fall of 1994. The purpose of this study was to identify work-related issues that contribute to their morale, either negatively or positively. The population surveyed consisted of all 1293 members of this administrative group employed in the University of Hawai'i ten campus system. There were 901 surveys returned for a response rate of 70%.

SUMMARY OF FINDINGS

Respondents were asked a variety of questions to determine those professional and institutional issues that are important to their morale as well as the overall level of their morale. Demographic information was used to determine whether specific issues or overall morale differ by gender, race/ethnicity, pay level, institutional type and/or mobility.

Institutional Issues Considered Most Important to APTs:

Salaries. APTs indicate that their salaries have a negative impact on their morale. They perceive that their salaries are low relative to their responsibilities and workload.

Opportunity for Promotions. Many APTs feel there are few opportunities for promotion and no clearly defined steps for advancement.

Opportunity for Career Development. APTs want management and personnel training to support their career growth and development. They specifically mentioned their desire for career-related workshops, conferences, computer training, and support of their graduate education and research.

Professional Issues Considered Most Important to APTs:

Degree of trust from their supervisor. APTs expect their supervisors to demonstrate confidence in their abilities and expertise to make sound decisions.

A sense of teamwork. APTs value teamwork that fosters cohesiveness and a sense of common purpose among and between work units.

Recognition for contribution. The APTs want to be recognized for their efforts to accomplish the goals of their work units and to make a notable contribution to the university.

Overall Morale:

- An overall morale score was calculated with a range of 1 to 15. The mean composite morale of the APTs (mean = 9.79) is above the mid-point of the range (mid-point = 8.0).

- There is no significant difference in overall morale by gender, ethnicity/race or pay level.

- There is a significant difference in overall morale by campus. APTs at Manoa had the lowest overall morale, and APTs at community colleges had the highest overall morale.

- There were significant differences in overall morale relative to perceived mobility. If APTs feel stuck in their position or intend to leave their current position, their overall morale is significantly lower than those who do not feel stuck or do not intend to leave.

Factors That Explain Overall Morale:

The survey included 53 professional and institutional issues. To create more reliable measures, the 53 items were reduced by factor analysis to nine factors, five institutional factors (career support, working conditions, discrimination, review/intervention, and diversity), and four professional factors (recognition for competence, gender/race issues, intra-department relations, external relations).

A multivariate regression was performed to determine which of the demographic and work-related factors explain overall morale. The results of the analysis indicate that APTs' perceptions of the career support and recognition for competence they receive, the relations external to the APTs department they experience, and the level of discrimination they perceive are significant predictors of their morale. The more positive these perceptions are, the more positive their morale. Feeling stuck or intending to leave their current position are significant negative indicators of overall morale. Of the demographic variables, only employment at a community college is a significant and positive predictor of morale.

Recommendations

There is substantial evidence that morale is important to employee satisfaction, retention and performance. Although the APTs who responded to this survey indicate a more positive than negative level of overall morale, these findings also identify specific means to enhance their morale:

- Clarify career paths that provide the means for advancement of APTs.

- Establish ways of recognizing the contributions of APTs.

- Review the job classification and compensation system.

- Foster the development of APT management and leadership skills.

- Identify and eliminate bureaucratic red tape.

- Provide workshops specifically designed to enhance team building and communication.

THE UNIVERSITY OF HAWAI'I SYSTEM ADMINISTRATIVE, PROFESSIONAL AND TECHNICAL STAFF MORALE STUDY

A morale survey was distributed to members of the Administrative, Professional and Technical (APT) staff at the University of Hawai'i to determine those work-related issues that contribute to their morale, either negatively or positively. All members of the APT system-wide staff were included. The instrument was mailed to 1293 members of this administrative group in the fall of 1994. There were 901 surveys returned for a response rate of 70%. Analyses were conducted on 869 surveys; the remaining 32 instruments were not useable. All individual responses are confidential; the findings are reported in broad patterns only.

The data were analyzed with three questions in mind. First, what work-related issues are important to the morale of APTs? Second, what is the overall morale of APTs and does it differ by gender, race/ethnicity, campus or pay level? Third, what combination of demographic and work-related variables explain the overall morale of APTs?

SUMMARY OF THE FINDINGS

Demographic Data on Respondents

Table 1 (on page 66) provides the demographic data on the respondents. Percentages do not total 100% due to missing data.

Position/job title. The three most prevalent position/job title categories held by respondents were educational specialists (186 or 21.4%), administrative officers (173 or 19.9%), and research associates (99 or 11.4%).

Race/ethnicity. The race/ethnicity reported by respondents indicates that 339 (39.0%) are Japanese, 225 (25.9%) are Caucasian, and 68 (7.8%) are Chinese.

Gender. Of the respondents who provided this information, gender was fairly balanced with 436 (50.2%) females and 414 (47.6%) males responding.

Age. There were 279 (32.1%) respondents in each of the age ranges of 22-35 years and 36-45 years. The third range, 46-55 years, included 189 individuals (21.7%). The remaining respondents were over 55 or didn't respond to the question.

Years of employment. The majority of the employees (428 or 49.2%) have been employed at UH from 1-5 years. The second largest group, those with 6-10 years of service, includes 173 (20.0%) respondents, and the third group, 11-20 years, includes 146 (16.8%).

Pay level. APT pay levels were grouped as follows: level one (01-04) included 133 (15.3%) of the respondents, and level two (05-08) represented the largest group with 300 (34.6%) individuals. Level three (09-12) consisted of 201 (23.1%) APT, and the final level, (13-17) included 52 (5.9%). Of the total APT respondents, 183 (21.1%) omitted information regarding their pay level.

Campus. The respondents represented 10 different campuses. Of the total, 650 (74.8%) APTs were from UH-Manoa, 120 (13.7%) were from community colleges, and 47 (5.4%) from UH-Hilo and UH-West Oahu.

Rank Order of Work-related Issues

Table 2 (on page 68) provides a list of work-related issues respondents selected as the three most important (from the total of 53 items on the instrument). Cumulative percent is the total percentage of respondents who indicated the issue was their first, second or third choice as most important. The most important institutional issues were salary, opportunity for promotions, and opportunity for career development (cumulative percents of 49.4, 45.6, and 35.8 respectively). Professional issues selected as the most important are the degree of trust demonstrated by supervisor, a sense of teamwork, and recognition for contribution (cumulative percents of 33.5, 22.0, and 21.6 respectively). The overall most important issues from both areas were salary (49.4%), opportunity for promotions (45.6%), and opportunity for career development (35.8%).

Nine Morale Factors Extracted for Comparisons

Respondents were asked to rate each of the 53 items on the survey in terms of its degree of impact on their morale. The scale extended from 1 to 5 (1 = negative impact and 5 = positive impact). The items which represented each of the two survey topics (institutional was comprised of 25 items and professional comprised of 28 items) were subjected to a factor analysis in order to reduce the data and provide more reliable measures. The goal of the factor analysis was to reduce the data to the least number of factors that made sense conceptually. Both orthogonal and oblique rotations were performed on both dimensions to determine the best fit. The results of the two rotations were virtually identical. The oblique rotations were retained for analyses.

Institutional dimensions. The factor analysis of the institutional dimensions resulted in a five factor loading displayed in Table 3 (on page 69). The labels we assigned to each factor appear in bold face. The alpha coefficients calculated for each factor were .85, .73, .79, .71 and .83, respectively. All factors were retained and considered reliable for further analysis.

Seven items loaded on the first factor. The items included: hiring practices, opportunity for career development, clear performance criteria, opportunity for promotions, workload distribution, support for professional activities, and hiring of external candidates, which seem to represent a dimension we chose to call the career support experienced by APTs. Six items loaded on the second factor: parking, work environment, university reputation, retirement plans/benefits, revenue/resources for unit, and salary. Collectively, these seem to represent the working conditions experienced by APTs. Four items loaded on the third factor: age, sex, ethnic discrimination, and staff turnover. These items seem to represent the discrimination perceived by APTs. Five items loaded on the fourth factor: federal government mandates, state government intervention, budget and program reviews, and bureaucratic red tape. This factor seems to represent the review/intervention experienced by the APTs. Two items loaded on the final and fifth factor: ethnic and gender diversity. The factor is labeled diversity.

Professional dimensions. The factor analysis of professional dimensions resulted in a five factor loading. One factor was dropped with an alpha of .68. Table 4 (on page 70) displays the remaining four factors with alpha coefficients of .91, .89, .84 and .72, respectively. The remaining factors were considered reliable for the purpose of further analysis.

Table 1

NUMBER AND PERCENT OF APT RESPONDENTS BY DEMOGRAPHIC VARIABLES
N=869

DEMOGRAPHICS	#	%
Position/Job Title		
Computer Specialist	72	8.3
Publication Specialist	39	4.5
Administrative Officers	173	19.9
Educational Specialists	186	21.4
Research Associates	99	11.4
Engineers and Related	34	3.9
Athletic Coaches	16	1.8
Technical and Professional	47	5.4
Other	86	9.9
Blank	117	13.5
Race/Ethnicity		
African-American	6	.7
Caucasian	225	25.9
Chinese	68	7.8
Filipino	33	3.8
Hawaiian	44	5.1
Hispanic	6	.7
Japanese	339	39.0
Korean	9	1.0
Native American	3	3.0
Samoan	0	.0
Asian	27	3.1
Other	33	3.8
Blank	76	8.7
Gender		
Female	436	50.2
Male	414	47.6
Blank	19	2.2
Age		
22-35	279	32.1
36-45	279	32.1
46-55	189	21.7
56-65	45	5.2
66+	6	.7
Blank	71	8.2

Table 1 (continued)

DEMOGRAPHICS	#	%
Years Employed		
01 - 05	428	49.2
06 - 10	173	20.0
11 - 20	146	16.8
21 - 30	84	9.6
31 +	2	.2
Blank	36	4.2
Pay Level		
01 - 04	133	15.3
05 - 08	300	34.6
09 - 12	201	23.1
13 - 17	52	5.9
Blank	183	21.1
Campus Employed		
University of Hawai'i - Manoa	650	74.8
University of Hawai'i - Hilo/West O'ahu	47	5.4
Hilo	45	5.2
West O'ahu	2	.2
Community Colleges	120	13.7
Hawai'i	5	.6
Honolulu	33	3.8
Kapi'olani	23	2.6
Kaua'i	7	.8
Leeward	23	2.6
Maui	20	2.3
Windward	6	.7
Other	22	2.5
Blank	30	3.5

Table 2

MOST IMPORTANT MORALE ISSUES AS REPORTED BY APTs

Institutional Issues	First	Second	Third	*Cumulative
25. Salary	24.3	13.1	12.0	49.4
03. Opportunity for promotions	15.2	20.0	10.4	45.6
02. Opport. career development	14.8	11.9	9.1	35.8
01. Support for prof. activities	7.0	4.9	5.3	17.2
07. Workload distribution	4.7	7.1	4.6	16.4
13. Bureaucratic red tape	2.4	4.0	4.7	11.1

Professional Issues	First	Second	Third	*Cumulative
32. Degree trust from supervisor	19.2	8.1	6.2	33.5
43. Sense of teamwork	6.4	6.6	9.0	22.0
34. Recognition for contribution	6.3	7.5	7.8	21.6
33. Recognition for expertise	7.6	9.0	3.5	20.1
37. Communication/supervisor	5.8	7.2	4.9	17.9
51. Authority to make decisions	5.3	5.1	5.4	15.8
29. Relationship with students	5.2	3.8	2.1	11.1

Top Five Issues	First	Second	Third	Cumulative
Salary	24.3	13.1	12.0	49.4
Opportunity for promotions	15.2	20.0	10.4	45.6
Opport. for career development	14.8	11.9	9.1	35.8
Degree of trust from supervisor	19.2	8.1	6.2	33.5
Sense of teamwork	6.4	6.6	9.0	22.0

* Cumulative percentage > 11%

Table 3

SUMMARY OF FACTOR ANALYSIS ON APT INSTITUTIONAL ISSUES
(STANDARDIZED REGRESSION COEFFICIENTS)

Institutional Issues	Factor Loading				
	1	2	3	4	5
Career Support					
Hiring practices	.79				
Opportunity for career development	.78				
Clear performance criteria	.76				
Opportunity for promotions	.72				
Workload distribution	.69				
Support for professional activities	.68				
Hiring of external candidates	.64				
Working Conditions					
Parking		.78			
Work environment		.69			
University reputation		.63			
Retirement plans/benefits		.57			
Revenue/resources for unit		.53			
Salary		.44			
Discrimination					
Age discrimination			.83		
Sex discrimination			.80		
Ethnic discrimination			.78		
Staff turnover			.61		
Review/Intervention					
Federal government mandates				.78	
State government intervention				.77	
Budget reviews				.53	
Program reviews				.51	
Bureaucratic red tape				.48	
Diversity					
Ethnic diversity					.89
Gender diversity					.88
	1	2	3	4	5
Mean =	3.18	3.26	2.66	2.52	3.49
Alpha =	.85	.73	.79	.71	.83

Table 4

SUMMARY OF FACTOR ANALYSIS ON APT PROFESSIONAL ISSUES
(STANDARDIZED REGRESSION COEFFICIENTS)

Professional Issues	Factor Loading			
	1	2	3	4
Recognition for Competence				
Recognition for contribution	.87			
Recognition for expertise	.86			
Degree of trust from supervisor	.86			
Communication from supervisor	.80			
Sufficient guidance	.79			
Feedback on performance	.66			
Pressures to perform	.58			
Authority to make decisions	.55			
Availability of mentoring	.45			
Relationship with sr. administrators	.41			
Leadership of your unit	.40			
Gender/Race Issues				
Racial/Ethnic harassment		.92		
Sex role stereotyping		.92		
Racial/Ethnic stereotyping		.92		
Sexual harassment		.88		
Department politics		.60		
Intra Department Relations				
Within department relations			.88	
Cross-department relations			.78	
Co-workers performance			.73	
Communication between units			.58	
Sense of teamwork			.56	
External Relations				
Relationship with the public				.84
Relationship with students				.81
Relationship with faculty				.66
	1	2	3	4
Mean =	3.48	2.50	3.45	3.90
Alpha =	.91	.89	.84	.72

Eleven items loaded on the first factor. These items included recognition for contribution, recognition for expertise, degree of trust from supervisor, communication from supervisor, sufficient guidance, feedback on performance, pressures to perform, authority to make decisions, availability of mentoring, relationship with senior administrators, and leadership of unit which seem to represent the recognition for competence experienced by APTs. Five items loaded on the second factor: racial/ethnic and sexual harassment, racial/ethnic and sex role stereotyping, and department politics. These issues seem to be the gender/race issues perceived by APTs. Five items loaded on the third factor: within department and cross-department relations, co-workers performance, communication between units, and sense of teamwork which seem to represent the intra-department relations experienced by APTs. Three items loaded on the fourth and final factor: relationship with the public, students, and faculty. These three items are simply labeled external relations.

In summary, the 53 work related items contributing to the morale experienced by APTs have been reduced to nine factors: career support, working conditions, discrimination, review/intervention, diversity, recognition for competence, gender/race issues, intra-department relations and external relations.

Table 5 (on page 72) provides the frequencies and percentages of the responses on the work-related issues by factor. The values are reported as a range from "-2" for negative impact to "+2" for positive impact. The values of the individual items are provided to demonstrate the pattern of the loadings as well as the relative importance of each item to the morale of APTs. Both extremes—most positive and most negative—indicate items that are important to morale.

Composite Morale Score

In order to examine the overall morale of APTs, three sets of questions were asked. First, the respondents were specifically asked to indicate their level of morale with respect to their experience on their campus. Again a Likert scale of "1" to "5" was used with "1" indicating low morale, "3" the midpoint, and "5" indicating high morale. The overall mean for APTs on this single measure was 3.15 with a standard deviation of .99.

Second, a set of questions were asked dealing with the values, caring, and fairness of the institution. On a five point scale, respondents indicated their degree of agreement with "1" representing strongly disagree, and "5" representing strongly agree. And finally, a third set of statements pertained to the variety, purpose, freedom, and satisfaction APTs experience on the job.

Responses to these three sets of questions were combined into a composite morale score with a range of 1-15 (the minimum is 3.98, and the maximum is 14.80). The midpoint is 8. The alpha coefficient on the composite score is .78. The mean composite morale of the APTs is 9.79 (SD=2.17).

Significant Differences on Overall Morale by Demographic Groups

Gender. Table 6 (on page 75) provides the means and standard deviations for female and male APTs on overall morale. There was no significant difference in overall morale by gender.

Race/ethnicity. Analysis of variance was used to determine whether overall morale differed by race or ethnicity as displayed in Table 7 (on page 75). Due to the small numbers in some groups, three groups were created for the purpose of this analysis: Caucasian (n=225), Asian (n=443) and Underrepresented (n=92). The underrepresented group includes African Americans, Filipinos, Hawaiians, Hispanics and Native Americans. There was no significant difference in overall morale by race/ethnicity.

Table 5

FREQUENCIES AND PERCENTAGES OF APT RESPONSES ON INSTITUTIONAL AND PROFESSIONAL ISSUES BY TOTAL RESPONDENTS

INSTITUTIONAL ISSUES	-2 #	-2 %	-1 #	-1 %	Value 0.0 #	0.0 %	+1 #	+1 %	+2 #	+2 %
Career Support										
Hiring practices	98	13	121	15	304	39	161	21	97	12
Opportunity for career development	95	11	137	16	156	18	203	24	258	30
Clear performance criteria	89	11	128	15	260	31	210	25	151	18
Opportunity for promotions	210	25	153	18	133	16	136	16	214	25
Workload distribution	110	13	159	19	253	30	199	24	121	14
Support for professional activities	59	7	109	14	203	25	221	27	212	26
Hiring of external candidates	76	11	107	15	334	48	134	19	43	6
Working Conditions										
Parking	135	17	113	14	219	27	166	21	165	21
Physical work environment	78	9	116	13	222	26	245	28	199	23
University reputation	34	4	83	10	354	42	259	31	115	14
Retirement plans/benefits	38	5	74	9	240	29	263	32	207	25
Revenue/resources for unit	120	15	164	20	221	27	195	24	122	15
Salary	166	19	204	24	198	23	159	18	135	16
Discrimination										
Age discrimination	102	16	101	16	306	48	74	12	59	9
Sex discrimination	164	24	137	20	274	41	57	8	39	6
Ethnic diversity of staff	29	4	41	5	340	44	196	26	160	21
Staff turnover	94	12	180	24	312	41	124	16	46	6
Review/Intervention										
Federal government mandates	79	12	153	24	338	53	48	8	17	3
State government intervention	159	22	222	31	270	38	40	6	16	2
Budget reviews	61	8	179	25	318	44	126	18	35	5
Program reviews	42	6	129	18	370	51	148	20	41	6
Bureaucratic red tape	442	52	237	28	119	14	28	3	17	2
Diversity										
Ethnic diversity	29	4	41	5	340	44	196	26	160	21
Gender diversity	30	4	63	8	354	46	190	25	130	17

Table 5 (continued)

PROFESSIONAL ISSUES	-2 #	-2 %	-1 #	-1 %	Value 0.0 #	Value 0.0 %	+1 #	+1 %	+2 #	+2 %
Recognition for competence										
Recognition for contribution	73	8	103	12	151	18	258	30	277	32
Recognition for expertise	56	7	98	11	136	16	281	33	287	33
Degree of trust from supervisor	53	6	57	7	106	12	205	24	443	51
Communication from supervisor	82	9	118	14	185	21	268	31	207	24
Sufficient guidance	65	8	123	15	237	28	267	32	153	18
Feedback on performance	74	9	122	15	220	27	255	31	155	19
Pressures to perform	86	10	133	16	376	46	166	20	60	7
Authority to make decisions	53	6	70	8	152	18	311	37	260	31
Availability of mentoring	85	12	128	18	288	40	140	19	79	11
Relationship with Sr. administrators	58	7	102	12	234	29	265	32	159	19
Leadership of your unit	85	10	77	9	250	30	241	29	170	21
Gender/Race Issues										
Racial/Ethnic harassment	143	24	94	16	270	45	55	9	42	7
Sex role stereotyping	147	23	120	19	274	43	54	9	38	6
Racial/Ethnic stereotyping	131	20	120	19	294	46	55	9	41	6
Sexual harassment	159	28	81	14	249	43	53	9	33	6
Department politics	242	30	249	31	223	28	60	7	31	4
Intra Department Relations										
Within department relations	40	5	75	9	247	28	308	35	166	19
Cross-department relations	31	4	85	10	330	38	267	31	100	12
Co-workers performance	33	4	74	9	251	29	310	36	159	18
Communication between units	84	10	151	17	274	32	195	22	110	13
Sense of teamwork	71	8	115	13	159	18	269	31	233	27
External Relations										
Relationship with the public	6	1	18	2	223	29	308	41	204	27
Relationship with students	6	1	19	3	171	23	275	37	275	37
Relationship with faculty	28	4	60	8	209	27	290	37	201	26

Campus. Table 8 (on page 75) provides the means and standard deviations on overall morale by campus. For the purpose of this analysis, the institutions were grouped as follows: Manoa, Hilo/West Oahu and the Community Colleges. All three groups indicated that overall campus morale was relatively positive ($\bar{X}$>8.0). However, the community colleges composite morale score ($\bar{X}$=10.37) is significantly more positive than that of Hilo/West Oahu ($\bar{X}$=9.91) and Manoa ($\bar{X}$=9.69).

Pay Level. Analysis was also conducted to determine whether morale differed by pay levels. The seventeen levels were divided into four pay level ranges as shown in Table 9 (on page 75). There was no significant difference in overall morale by pay level.

Perceived Mobility. Two specific questions were asked of the APTs regarding their mobility: whether they feel stuck in their positions and whether they intend to leave their current position. Table 10 (on page 75) provides the means and standard deviations on their overall morale. The data indicate that APTs who feel stuck or intend to leave their current position have significantly lower overall morale ($\bar{X}$=8.93, 8.63, respectively) than those who do not feel stuck or do not intend to leave ($\bar{X}$=10.65, 10.37, respectively).

Multivariate Regression of Selected Variables on Morale. Four models were constructed to explain overall morale. (Correlations between the variables were determined and are displayed in Table 11 on page 77.) The first model included the demographic factors of pay level, age, gender, ethnicity and institutional type (See Table 12 on page 78). Of the five variables included in this model, age and institutional type are significant (p<.001) in explaining the variance in morale. Of the institutional types, only employment in a community college is significant. Pay level, ethnicity and gender are not significant factors that predict morale in this model or subsequent models. This model explains only 4 percent of the variance (adjusted R^2=.04).

In the second model, institutional factors were added: career support, working conditions, discrimination, program review/intervention, and diversity to determine whether they contributed to the explained variance. Four factors (career support, working conditions, discrimination, and diversity) are significant (p=.03). Program review/intervention was not significant in predicting morale in this model or subsequent models. The demographics, age and institutional type, maintained their significance (p=.001) and were not suppressed with the addition of the institutional factors. The second model explained 28 percent of the variance in morale (adjusted R^2=.28).

The third model includes the professional factors: recognition for competence, gender/race issues, intra-department relations, and external relations. These were added to the demographics and the institutional factors to determine whether they would further explain variance in morale. Two factors were significant: recognition for competence and external relations (p<.001). The factors that did not significantly predict variance in this or the final model were gender/race issues and intra-department relations. Again the demographics, age and institutional type, remained significant (p<.02). The institutional factors of career support and discrimination maintained their ability to predict morale (p=.01), but working conditions and diversity are no longer significant in this model. The third model explains 43 percent of the variance in morale (adjusted R^2=.43).

The fourth and final model includes the perceived mobility of respondents as expressed by feeling stuck or intent to leave their current position. This model includes all the variables, demographic, institutional, professional, and perceived mobility. Both feeling stuck and intent

Table 6

MEANS AND STANDARD DEVIATION ON OVERALL APT MORALE BY GENDER

	Female		Male			
	$\bar{X}$	SD	$\bar{X}$	SD	t	*p
Composite Morale Score	9.74	2.11	9.82	2.23	-.55	.59
	N=436		N=414			

*Significance of t-ratio

Table 7

MEANS AND STANDARD DEVIATION ON OVERALL APT MORALE BY RACE/ETHNICITY

	Caucasian		Asian		Underrepresented**			
	$\bar{X}$	SD	$\bar{X}$	SD	$\bar{X}$	SD	F	*p
Composite Morale Score	10.04	2.21	9.68	2.09	9.78	2.28	2.07	.13
	N=225		N=443		N=92			

*Significance of analysis of variance
**Underrepresented includes: African Americans, Filipinos, Hawaiians, Hispanics, and Native Americans

Table 8

MEANS AND STANDARD DEVIATION ON OVERALL APT MORALE BY CAMPUS

	Manoa		Hilo/WO		Comm. Colleges			
	$\bar{X}$	SD	$\bar{X}$	SD	$\bar{X}$	SD	F	*p
Composite Morale Score	9.69	2.11	9.91	2.31	10.37	2.21	5.96	.003
	N=650		N-47		N=142			

*Significance of analysis of variance

Table 9

MEANS AND STANDARD DEVIATION ON OVERALL APT MORALE BY PAY LEVEL

	Level 01 - 04		Level 05 - 08		Level 09 - 12		Level 13 - 17			
	$\bar{X}$	SD	$\bar{X}$	SD	$\bar{X}$	SD	$\bar{X}$	SD	F	*p
Composite Morale Score	9.91	2.15	9.72	2.06	9.92	2.14	9.77	2.36	.48	.70
	N=133		N=300		N-201		N=52			

*Significance of analysis of variance

Table 10

MEANS AND STANDARD DEVIATION ON OVERALL APT MORALE BY PERCEIVED MOBILITY

	Feeling Stuck						Intent to Leave					
	yes		no				yes		no			
	$\bar{X}$	SD	$\bar{X}$	SD	t	*p	$\bar{X}$	SD	$\bar{X}$	SD	t	*p
Composite Morale Score	8.93	2.10	10.65	1.88	-12.8	.00	8.63	2.00	10.37	2.04	-11.7	.00
	N=418		N=415				N=273		N-558			

*Significance of t-ratio

to leave their current position are significant (p=.00). The professional factors: recognition for competence and external relations maintained their strength in predicting morale (p=.00). The institutional factors: career support and discrimination also remained significant (p<.01). And finally, institutional type, specifically employment in a community college, remained significant (p=.00). Age, however, is no longer significant in the final model with the addition of the mobility issues of feeling stuck and intent to leave. The final model explains 51 percent of the variance (adjusted R^2=.51).

Although pay level, ethnicity, gender, program review/intervention, gender/race issues, and intra-department relations were not significant factors in predicting morale for this population, attempts to drop any of these variables resulted in reducing the variance explained, indicating that all the variables in the final model play a role in explaining overall morale.

Qualitative Data

The final open-ended question on the survey asked what kind of staff development or training would be most helpful to the APTs. Ten specific areas of training and development were identified as most important. The numbers in the parentheses represent the number of respondents who mentioned the item in response to this question.

1. Personnel and supervisory/management training (108). (e.g., how to deal with the poor performer or ineffective worker; progressive discipline process).

2. Support career growth and development through attendance at workshops, conferences, and seminars—locally or nationally (82).

3. Computer training (79). Respondents wanted to get more out of their software applications.

4. Enhancement of both the unit and institutional communication skills and development (29).

5. Support and encouragement to pursue graduate education and research (28).

6. Time management and organizational skills to improve efficiency and production (25).

7. Orientation to university policies and procedures (24).

8. Business and grant writing (20).

9. Procurement procedures and policies (20).

Table 11

CORRELATIONS* AMONG SELECTED DEMOGRAPHIC VARIABLES, EXTRACTED FACTORS AND OVERALL APT MORALE

	Campus	Gender	Age	Pay	Work	Discrim	Diversity	Carsupp	Review	Deptrel	Extrel	Genrace	Recogn	Stuck	Leave
Gender	.03														
Age	.07	.09													
Pay leve	-.14	.21	.33												
Work	.04	.01	.06	.01											
Discrim	.05	.09	.17	-.02	-.01										
Diversity	.05	-.02	-.03	-.08	.17	.11									
Carsupp	-.03	-.01	-.06	-.06	.55	-.07	.15								
Review	-.00	.01	.07	.01	.26	.30	.13	.29							
Deptrel	-.01	-.06	.07	-.03	.44	.09	.25	.50	.24						
Extrel	.08	-.04	.07	-.10	.26	.02	.31	.21	.14	.43					
Genrace	.11	.08	.20	.02	-.07	.64	.13	-.15	.17	.02	.08				
Recogn	.02	-.01	.06	-.02	.45	.06	.19	.61	.27	.66	.34	-.00			
Stuck	.05	-.01	.04	-.01	.16	.03	.17	.22	.07	.25	.11	.06	.25		
Leave	.02	.02	.18	.12	.12	.06	.09	.11	.14	.12	.07	.09	.19	.24	
Morale	.14	.05	.16	.00	.35	.20	.22	.41	.24	.47	.34	.17	.57	.35	.38

N = 637

*Strength of correlations is interpreted as follows:

.01 - .1 = very low
.2 - .3 = low
.4 - .5 = moderate
.6 - .7 = substantial
.8 - .9 = very high

Table 12

MULTIVARIATE REGRESSION OF SELECTED VARIABLES ON OVERALL APT MORALE

VARIABLES	Model #1				Model #2				Model #3				Model #4			
	b	SE b	Beta	p*	b	SE b	Beta	p*	b	SE b	Beta	p*	b	SE b	Beta	p*
Demographics																
Pay level	-.02	.03	-.03	.55	-.01	.03	-.02	.66	.00	.02	-.01	.87	-.02	.02	-.03	.42
Age	.03	.01	.17	.00**	.03	.01	.13	.00**	.02	.01	.08	.02*	.01	.01	.05	.17
Gender: Female	.22	.18	.05	.22	.11	.16	.03	.47	.18	.14	.04	.21	.19	.13	.04	.15
Ethnicity: Underrepresented	-.45	.38	-.05	.24	-.34	.33	-.04	.29	-.13	.30	-.01	.67	-.22	.27	-.02	.42
Institutional type: Community colleges	.91	.24	.16	.00**	.88	.21	.15	.00**	.80	.19	.14	.00**	.76	.18	.13	.00**
Institutional Factors																
Career Support					.87	.11	.35	.00**	.32	.11	.13	.01*	.28	.11	.12	.01*
Working conditions					.26	.12	.10	.03*	.07	.11	.02	.54	.04	.10	.01	.72
Discrimination					.44	.11	.16	.00**	.30	.12	.11	.01*	.36	.11	.13	.00**
Review/intervention					.14	.15	.04	.37	.04	.14	.01	.77	.02	.13	.01	.85
Diversity					.33	.09	.14	.00**	.13	.08	.05	.12	.05	.08	.02	.55
Professional Factors																
Recog. for competence									.98	.12	.39	.00**	.85	.11	.38	.00**
Gender/racial issues									.10	.11	.04	.38	-.00	.10	-.00	.98
Intra depart. relations									.12	.12	.05	.32	.09	.11	.04	.42
External relations									.40	.12	.13	.00**	.43	.11	.14	.00**
Perceived Mobility																
Stuck in position													.70	.13	.16	.00**
Intent to leave													1.05	.14	.23	.00**
Adjusted R-squared	.04				.28				.43				.51			
F Ratio	4.17				26.05				32.68				40.80			

*p<.01   **p <.001

10. Campus and site visits with peers in similar positions (20).

Numerous additional comments were made by the APTs. A representative sample of these comments appears later in this chapter.

Recommendations

Although the APTs who responded to this survey indicate a more positive than negative level of overall morale, these findings also identify specific means to enhance their morale:

- Clarify career paths that provide the means for advancement of APTs. Feeling stuck in a position with little expectation of mobility is a significant contributor to low morale.

- Establish ways of recognizing the contributions of APTs to their work units and to the University as a whole. Supervisors need to express appreciation for a job well done and recognition for the quality of the effort expended.

- Review the job classification and compensation system to ensure that it is based on performance and workload distribution. Many APTs want performance appraisals which reward performance based on merit. One specific issue that causes tension is the lack of parity with those in other classifications performing essentially the same tasks.

- Foster the development of APT management and leadership skills. These should include supervisory and management techniques, personnel policies and legal guidelines that relate to their responsibilities.

- Identify and eliminate bureaucratic red tape and/or regulations that create unnecessary work. Incentives could be instituted to find creative ways to streamline work and save time and money.

- Provide workshops specifically designed to enhance team building and communication between APTs, their supervisors and co-workers.

Conclusion

This study identified numerous issues the members of the Administrative, Professional, and Technical staff consider important to their morale. The majority of the staff responded to the survey, and many provided thoughtful and constructive comments on how to improve the quality of worklife at the University of Hawai'i. It is important to emphasize that improving the quality of worklife serves the University as well as it serves individual staff members. There is substantial evidence that morale is important to employee satisfaction, retention and performance. The overall morale of APTs is not low, but there is much that could be done to improve it. APTs are important to the optimum functioning of the University, and the quality of their worklives deserves attention.

REPRESENTATIVE COMMENTS FROM APT SURVEYS

All comments made on the surveys were tallied and representative comments are quoted below. Comments were made by approximately 50% of the respondents, and the overwhelming majority of these comments addressed work-related issues that have a negative impact on the current morale of APTs. The comments are categorized by the relevant factor, and the number commenting on the particular institutional or professional issue are indicated. Only those factors that received comments from more than 25 respondents are included.

Career Support
(Of the respondents, 283 made comments on the need for career support. Of those, 140 specifically addressed the need for promotion opportunity.)

Almost zero opportunity for career advancement for APTs.

How do we move in the system or get promoted? Upgrading is such a difficult and lengthy process.

It would enhance my job performance if I was able to participate in professional activities. There is no career development.

Career development is important—improved performance criteria would improve morale with APTs.

The constant availability of positions for promotions is a big positive of the APT classification.

Promotions in the unit are nonexistent. I am forced to leave a good environment in order to be promoted, since upgrading my existing position is not possible.

Do not have a clear idea of what my job entails; changes are made without any notice or discussion about what the impact is.

There is no promotion system. Most people tend to underestimate the knowledge and skill to perform our job.

Workload should be evenly distributed. No clear performance criteria leaves employee without clear goals. Employees draw their own conclusions about work performance and capabilities.

Supervisor will not allow me to take classes during the day. Policy is not uniformly applied.

I have had ample opportunity for developing technical and administrative skills. But I have little opportunity for promotions or raises given the current class/structure.

I am interested in advancement opportunities in order to make a living wage in a job that gives me employment and satisfaction. These are the basic human needs and desires. The need to know what is expected of you, whether you are meeting or exceeding expectations and whether the department is bound in the same goals and directions.

Lack of professional development causes low morale and staff turnover.

Working Conditions
(Of the respondents, 245 made comments on the quality of working conditions. Of those, 164 specifically addressed salary.)

Need to pay for APT contribution.

I consider the taking of courses from the university one of the most important benefits of working here. It allows a person to better themselves.

I think having an APT and a faculty employee in the same office is a big mistake.

The retirement plan is below average and not worth putting a lot of years at this job.

Salaries do not meet the cost of living needs in Hawai'i.

I would like to see merit increases become possible.

I love my work environment, and the opportunity is there if I want it; a salary upgrade would be nice.

No pay increases to look forward to—although people in the same office get more money than I do for the same work.

Buildings are deteriorating.

Parking is not convenient, I often work late. I only feel stuck in terms of my salary.

Mostly a positive working experience.

Feeling safe is important to me because I am required to work early and late hours to meet deadlines.

I am trying hard not to feel burned out, but the feeling of being underpaid and overworked do surface from time to time.

Working with faculty specialists in the same job, but not the same pay, is not fair.

Compensation appears unrelated to performance—very discouraging. More appreciation is needed—I feel so taken for granted.

Review/Intervention
(Of the respondents, 73 made comments on the issues of program review and external intervention.)

We are buried in more and more useless forms, regulations and procedures to the point where real job performance is impossible.

There is so much red tape you can't do your job.

Reimbursements, hiring and initial paychecks are much too slow to the point of ridiculous.

Purchase order processing is excessive, bid lists are not always cost effective, each purchase order has different guidelines.

Program reviews are a farce, eliminate those programs that are a waste...the UH needs to thrive.

Paperwork is ridiculous!

Recognition for Competence
(Of the respondents, 258 made comments on the need for recognition and appreciation. Of those, 75 specifically addressed the need for trust from their supervisors.)

It's important that our supervisors trust us and believe in our work; we have no other form of job security.

There are no real rewards or recognition of work performed or contributions made to unit or institution.

Employees need to feel the support of their superiors in knowing they are doing a good job. Most problems evolve from lack of communication. Every employee will do his/her best if given the proper recognition and authority to make decisions within his/her expertise.

APTs do a lot of work often at the same level/capacity as higher administrators but receive little or no recognition. We are not thanked or recognized.

Unfortunately, there is no reward for excellent work; merit pay is still not available.

Too many APTs go unrewarded for years of excellent and loyal service—now they are working in the private sector.

We need to make employees feel important and recognize them for their work. In order to do good work, I need to trust my supervisor. We need to train these managers and supervisors to recognize and praise their workers to at least show them they're appreciated. For a lot of people even giving a compliment to others is difficult for them.

No recognition from administrators, No pats on the back, No support, and No encouragement on a job well done.

I really trust my supervisor highly and have a positive relationship. I am part of the planning and policy development of the department.

Please train the Senior Administrators.

My work progress is hampered by those who do not make timely decisions.

Sink or swim attitude from supervisor, never any performance feedback. I feel isolated from the rest of the system.

We play a major part in fulfilling the institution's mission but we are not given credit or recognition. I am comfortable in what I do. I have been an administrator for 20 years in the UH system but do not feel I have been fairly treated or respected for my work.

I need to have support and trust of my supervisor. I need some objective criticism, definite guidelines, and the freedom to make decisions.

Morale is low due to the lack of communication and organization from our supervisor. He brags about how he does everything himself and we are constantly scrambling.

Intra-Department Relations
(Of the respondents, 33 made comments on the importance of intra-department relations.)

There is not enough communication between departments.

Develop organization esprit de corps and increase cooperation within unit.

Each member of the team can contribute to the overall success of the team.

Let's work in a team rather than individually.

External Relations
(Of the respondents, 33 made comments on the importance of their relations with students, faculty and the public.)

It is essential that I communicate well with the faculty and students.

Students make the job personally satisfying.

It is essential that I communicate well with faculty and students.

Having a good relationship with faculty and getting recognized for work well done will help morale the most.

The more you do, the faculty member sees you as taking over their job. Institution supports the faculty not the APTs.

CONFIDENTIAL SURVEY OF THE UNIVERSITY

ADMINISTRATIVE, PROFESSIONAL AND

TECHNICAL STAFF (APTS)

This survey instrument has been developed to examine morale among administrative, professional and technical staff (APTS) at the University of Hawai'i. We describe morale as a state of mind regarding one's job. It includes satisfaction, commitment, loyalty and a sense of common purpose.

Please indicate the extent to which each of the following factors contribute to your morale by circling the appropriate number. For example, a response rate of "1" indicates that this factor has a negative impact on your morale. A response rate of "5" indicates that this factor has a positive impact on your morale. If the factor does not apply to you, indicate by circling N/A (not applicable).

At the end of each section we will ask you to provide the top three factors that affect your morale and to provide any additional comments.

Please rate these factors in terms of the degree of their impact on YOUR morale.						
	Negative Impact				Positive Impact	
	1	2	3	4	5	N/A

Institutional Factors

1. Support for professional activities	1	2	3	4	5	N/A
2. Opportunity for career development	1	2	3	4	5	N/A
3. Opportunity for promotions	1	2	3	4	5	N/A
4. Clear performance criteria	1	2	3	4	5	N/A
5. Hiring practices	1	2	3	4	5	N/A
6. Hiring for external candidates	1	2	3	4	5	N/A
7. Workload distribution	1	2	3	4	5	N/A
8. Staff turnover	1	2	3	4	5	N/A
9. Ethnic diversity of staff	1	2	3	4	5	N/A
10. Gender diversity of staff	1	2	3	4	5	N/A
11. Federal government mandates	1	2	3	4	5	N/A
12. State government intervention	1	2	3	4	5	N/A
13. Bureaucratic red tape	1	2	3	4	5	N/A
14. Institutional sex discrimination (subtle and/or overt)	1	2	3	4	5	N/A
15. Institutional racial/ethnic discrimination (subtle and/or overt)	1	2	3	4	5	N/A
16. Program reviews	1	2	3	4	5	N/A
17. Budget reviews						
18. Retirement plans/benefits	1	2	3	4	5	N/A

19.	Age discrimination	1	2	3	4	5	N/A
20.	Revenue/resources for your unit	1	2	3	4	5	N/A
21.	Parking	1	2	3	4	5	N/A
22.	Physical work environment	1	2	3	4	5	N/A
23.	Reputation of the University of Hawai'i	1	2	3	4	5	N/A
24.	Ethical conduct in unit	1	2	3	4	5	N/A
25.	Salary	1	2	3	4	5	N/A
26.	Other_____	1	2	3	4	5	N/A

27. Which of the factors listed above are most important to you as an APT?
    1st Important _____
    2nd Important _____
    3rd Important_____
    Please comment on these important factors:

    _____

    _____

    _____

    _____

Please rate these factors in terms of the degree of their impact on YOUR morale:

	Negative Impact			Positive Impact		
	1	2	3	4	5	N/A

Professional factors							
28.	Relationship with faculty	1	2	3	4	5	N/A
29.	Relationship with students	1	2	3	4	5	N/A
30.	Relationship with the public	1	2	3	4	5	N/A
31.	Relationship with senior administrators	1	2	3	4	5	N/A
32.	Degree of trust from supervisor	1	2	3	4	5	N/A
33.	Recognition for expertise	1	2	3	4	5	N/A
34.	Recognition for contribution	1	2	3	4	5	N/A
35.	Sufficient guidance	1	2	3	4	5	N/A
36.	Pressures to perform	1	2	3	4	5	N/A
37.	Communication from supervisors	1	2	3	4	5	N/A
38.	Communication between units	1	2	3	4	5	N/A
39.	Importance of my job to institution	1	2	3	4	5	N/A
40.	Co-workers performance	1	2	3	4	5	N/A
41.	Within departmental relationships	1	2	3	4	5	N/A
42.	Cross-department relations	1	2	3	4	5	N/A
43.	Sense of teamwork	1	2	3	4	5	N/A
44.	Racial/ethnic stereotyping	1	2	3	4	5	N/A
45.	Racial/ethnic harassment	1	2	3	4	5	N/A

46. Sex-role stereotyping	1	2	3	4	5	N/A
47. Sexual harassment	1	2	3	4	5	N/A
48. Department politics	1	2	3	4	5	N/A
49. Availability of mentoring	1	2	3	4	5	N/A
50. Feedback to performance	1	2	3	4	5	N/A
51. Authority to make decisions	1	2	3	4	5	N/A
52. Support from collective bargaining unit	1	2	3	4	5	N/A
53. Visibility in the organization	1	2	3	4	5	N/A
54. Leadership of your unit	1	2	3	4	5	N/A
55. Institutional leadership	1	2	3	4	5	N/A
56. Other_____	1	2	3	4	5	N/A

57. Which of the previous factors are most important to you as an APT?
    lst important_____
    2nd Important_____
    3rd Important_____
    Please comment on these important factors:

    _____

    _____

    _____

    _____

    _____

Please indicate your agreement with the following statements about your work.

	Strongly Disagree				Strongly Agree
58. There is too little variety in my job.	1	2	3	4	5
59. There's a common purpose in my unit.	1	2	3	4	5
60. There must be better places to work.	1	2	3	4	5
61. I would like more freedom on the job.	1	2	3	4	5
62. I am satisfied with the work I do.	1	2	3	4	5

Please indicate your agreement with the following statements about the institution.

	Strongly Disagree				Strongly Agree
63. I am loyal to the institution.	1	2	3	4	5
64. My opinions are valued.	1	2	3	4	5
65. This institution values its employees.	1	2	3	4	5
66. This institution is a caring organization.	1	2	3	4	5
67. This is a fair institution.	1	2	3	4	5

Please indicate your level of morale with respect to your experience on your campus.

Low morale   High morale

1   2   3   4   5

68. Do you have plans to leave your current position?

Yes_____No_____

69. Do you feel "stuck" in your position?

Yes_____No_____

Demographic information

70. At which campus are you employed?_____

71. What years have you been employed on your campus? 19_____ to 19_____

72. Which of the following most closely describes your administrative unit?

Academic Affairs_____   External Affairs_____

Student Affairs_____   Other (please specify)_____

Business/Facilities Affairs_____

73. Please state the title of your position/job: _____

74. What is your pay range? (01-17)   _____

75. What is your gender?   Female_____Male_____

76. What is the year of your birth?   _____

77. What is your race/ethnicity? (indicate group with which you most closely identify):

_____

78. In your work unit, are you a minority by gender?   Yes_____No_____

79. In your work unit, are you a minority by race or ethnicity?   Yes_____ No_____

80. What kind of staff development or training would be most helpful to you?

_____

_____

_____

_____

_____

Please feel free to provide any additional comments on the back of this page.

THANK YOU FOR YOUR TIME AND EFFORT!

Please return this survey in the enclosed envelope to:
Dr. Linda K. Johnsrud, Wist Hall, College of Education

Chapter 9

Case Study #2:

An Example of a University Faculty Morale Assessment

The case study presented in this chapter is also an authentic study that was conducted at the University of Hawaii at Manoa. In this case, the University of Hawaii at Manoa Faculty Senate had sponsored a morale survey every two years beginning in 1983. This chapter describes the process and the results of the 1993-94 effort.

Data Source

The University of Hawaii at Manoa is classified as a Carnegie Research University I emphasizing research and graduate education. The university is one of a select group of land, sea, and space grant institutions. The campus enrolls approximately 19,000 students, with about 4,000 pursuing graduate studies. Nearly 2,000 faculty are employed. The faculty are represented in collective bargaining by the University of Hawaii Professional Assembly.

The campus is one of the most diverse in the nation. About one-third (34.3 percent) of the undergraduates are Japanese, 17.8 percent are Caucasian, 11.1 percent are Chinese, 10.1 percent are Filipino, and 6.8 percent are Hawaiian. Nearly 70 percent of the faculty are Caucasian, recruited predominantly from mainland universities. The University of Hawaii at Manoa ranks among the leading American institutions of higher education in terms of numbers of foreign scholars on its staff and foreign students enrolled in its numerous colleges. Located in the capital city of Honolulu, a city with one of the highest costs of living in the United States, the University of Hawaii at Manoa has had difficulty recruiting and retaining faculty, particularly junior faculty.

Instrument Design

The original instrument used by the University of Hawaii at Manoa Senate since 1983 to survey faculty morale had been criticized by faculty because it did not sufficiently address the concerns of all faculty. The faculty represented by the Senate consist of instructional and research faculty, librarians, extension agents, and educational specialists. An ad hoc committee of faculty representing each of these groups assisted in the development of a new instrument. The development of the new instrument was based on a review of the literature and approved by the ad hoc committee.

Fifty-one items were clustered into nine scales: professional work life, reward/evaluation system, collegial relations, students, faculty governance, personal issues, support services, advocacy for faculty and leadership. The 81 items were arranged in a Likert format; that is, a response of "1" indicated the item had a negative effect on morale, a response of "3" indicated a neutral effect, and response of "5" indicated the item had a positive effect on morale. (Note that on the revised version in Appendix 3, we have changed the scale to range from -2 to +2 with 0 as the neutral point.) One question regarding overall change in morale was retained from the original survey to provide a means to compare current morale with that measured in earlier years.

The revised version of the instrument in Appendix 3 is the one we would use if we were going to conduct the assessment again. Another change from the original is the addition of a series of questions that provide a composite measure of morale. This additional measure provides a means to test a regression model to determine which of the work-related issues explain overall morale (as we did with the administrator morale assessment described in Chapter 8).

Procedures

The survey instrument was mailed to the total population of 1,956 faculty employed at the university. A series of three mailings was used to enhance the return rate. Samples of the cover letters for each of the mailings are included in Appendix 1. Each survey instrument was coded; however, individual names were never associated with individual responses and confidentiality was assured. The second mailing was a reminder notice sent to those who had not responded 10 days after the initial mailing. The third mailing, mailed 10 days after the second, included another reminder and another copy of the instrument. This process yielded a 53 percent response rate, considerably higher than previous years.

Findings of the Survey

The data were analyzed and a technical report was written for dissemination. The technical report is included in its entirety on the following pages.

FINDINGS OF THE 1993-94

SURVEY OF UH-MANOA

FACULTY MORALE

Sponsored by the UH-Manoa Faculty Senate

Principal Investigator:
Dr. Linda K. Johnsrud
Associate Professor of Education
Chair, UH-Manoa Senate 1993-94

Acknowledgments

Special thanks go to members of the ad hoc Committee on the Morale Survey who assisted in the revision and up-date of the instrument: Carol Anne Dickson, Chair; Geoffrey Ashton, John Carlson, James Cartwright, Linda Cox, and Adrienne Valdez. Thanks also go to Charlotte Mitsutani, Helen Yano and Cheryl Mori of the Manoa Faculty Senate staff for coordinating the survey distribution and data entry, and to Christine Des Jarlais for creating the tables.

THE 1993–94 SURVEY OF UH-MANOA FACULTY MORALE

The Manoa Faculty Senate has conducted a faculty morale survey six times in the last eleven years (1983, 1984, 1985, 1987, 1990 and 1992). This year the survey was substantially revised to better reflect the concerns of all members of the faculty (i.e. instructors, researchers, specialists, agents and librarians).

The revised instrument was mailed to the 1,956 members of the faculty in the spring of 1994. 1,036 surveys were returned for a 53% response rate. (This compares with 645 returned surveys in 1992.) Fourteen instruments were not useable; analyses were conducted on the remaining 1,022.

The data were analyzed with two questions in mind. First, what factors contribute to high and low levels of faculty morale? Second, are there differences by gender, race/ethnicity, tenure status, faculty classification, academic rank or locus of appointment?

Summary of the Findings

Demographic data on respondents

Table 1 provides the demographic data on the respondents. Comparative data available from 1992 indicate that response by academic rank has remained the same for assistant professors at 25.3% but that the response for associate professors has declined from 28.4% to 23.4%, and for full professors from 42.6% to 32.4%. (Absolute numbers have obviously increased.) Also the response by women was 22.1% in 1992 and now accounts for 33.4%. Note that 25.8% of the respondents did not report their race or ethnicity.

Descriptive data on all survey items

Table 2 provides the means and standard deviations on all items included on the survey. Respondents were asked to rate each item in terms of its impact on their morale. The scale was "1" for negative impact to "5" for positive impact. "3" is the mid-point of the scale.

Survey items were grouped by substantive area. Among the items on professional worklife, graduate and undergraduate teaching load ($\overline{X}$ = 3.85 and 3.44, respectively) have the most positive impact on morale with parking and availability of graduate assistants ($\overline{X}$ = 2.43 and 2.40, respectively) having the most negative impact. In regard to the reward and evaluation system, all means were below 3.0 with institutional rewards for teaching and service ranking the lowest ($\overline{X}$ = 2.51 and 2.50, respectively).

Collegial relations received generally high means on the survey with all items at 3.0 or higher with the exception of access to colleagues off campus ($\overline{X}$ = 2.94). Enthusiasm and ability of graduate students have a positive impact ($\overline{X}$ = 3.93 and 3.52) while the institutional support of both graduate and undergraduate students have a more negative impact ($\overline{X}$ = 2.74 and 2.73, respectively). Questions regarding faculty governance were aimed at the department, college and university levels. Items were perceived more negatively as one moves away from the department level, and budget decisions at all levels were a source of negative impact. Personal issues such as housing and standard of living have a negative impact on morale ($\overline{X}$ = 2.47 and 2.43, respectively). Support services received means ranging from a high of 3.24 for campus libraries to a low of 2.22 for facilities (repair and maintenance).

In regard to advocacy for faculty, respondents were asked to rate each entity in terms of its weakness or strength as an advocate ("1" indicating weak and "5" indicating strong). Chair or equivalent was perceived as

Table 1

NUMBER AND PERCENT OF FACULTY RESPONDENTS BY DEMOGRAPHIC VARIABLES
N=1022

DEMOGRAPHICS	NUMBER	PERCENT
FACULTY CLASSIFICATION		
Instructional	604	59.1
Researcher	121	11.8
Specialist	144	14.1
Librarian	29	2.8
Agent	29	2.8
Other	10	1.0
Blank	85	8.3
ACADEMIC RANK		
Instructor	56	5.5
Assistant	259	25.3
Associate	239	23.4
Full	331	32.4
Other	66	6.5
Blank	71	6.9
TENURE STATUS		
Yes, tenured	504	49.3
No, not tenured	453	44.3
Blank	65	6.4
APPOINTMENT		
9-month	427	41.8
11-month	500	48.9
Blank	95	9.3
AGE		
22-35	127	12.4
36-45	314	30.7
46-55	333	32.6
56-65	154	15.1
66+	27	2.6
Blank	67	6.6
GENDER		
Female	341	33.4
Male	615	60.2
Blank	66	6.5

Table 1 (continued)

DEMOGRAPHICS	NUMBER	PERCENT
RACE/ETHNICITY		
African-American	2	0.2
Caucasian	549	53.7
Chinese	42	4.1
Filipino	14	1.4
Hawaiian	18	1.8
Hispanic	7	0.7
Japanese	93	9.1
Korean	5	0.5
Native-American	4	0.4
Samoan	0	0
Other	24	2.3
Blank	264	25.8
LOCUS OF APPOINTMENT		
Colleges of Arts & Sciences:		
Arts & Humanities	75	7.3
Languages, Linguistics, & Literature	85	8.3
Natural Sciences	66	6.5
Social Sciences	66	6.5
College of Business Administrations	31	3.0
College of Continuing Education & Community Services	9	.9
College of Education	109	10.7
College of Engineering	25	2.4
College of Health Sciences & Social Welfare:		
School of Medicine	81	7.9
School of Nursing	26	2.5
School of Public Health	15	1.5
School of Social Work	13	1.3
College of Tropical Agriculture and Human Resources	138	13.5
School of Architecture	4	0.4
School of Law	6	0.6
School of Library Studies	2	0.2
Library Services	24	2.3
Organized Research Units & Academic Affairs	28	2.7
School of Ocean & Earth Science & Technology (SOEST)	70	6.8
School of Hawaiian, Asian, & Pacific Studies (SHAPS)	14	1.4
Student Affairs	24	2.3
School of Travel Industry Management	6	0.6
Split Appointments	33	3.2

the strongest advocate ($\overline{X}$ = 3.49), and as one moves away from the department, advocacy was perceived to weaken (i.e., from Dean to Central Administration to President to Board of Regents to Legislature to Governor ($\overline{X}$ = 2.97, 2.24, 2.09, 1.90, 1.84 and 1.77, respectively). Confidence in leadership reflected the same pattern with highest confidence in the Chair, and decreasing confidence as one moves away from the department.

Respondents were also asked to list the three items (among the total of 81 items on the instrument) that have the most negative impact on their morale and the three items with the most positive impact. No one item (positive or negative) received more than 24% (cumulative percentage) of the first, second or third choices indicating that to what faculty members attribute their morale is fairly idiosyncratic. The following received between 10% and 24% of the first, second or third choices:

Five most positive items:	Five most negative items:
Collegial relations with department	Current salary
Enthusiasm of graduate students	Standard of living
Enthusiasm of undergraduate students	Housing
Relations with department chair	Dean's leadership
Support for career from chair	Physical work environment

Nine morale scales created for comparisons

In order to make more refined comparisons by demographic differences, scales were created from each substantive set of items and analyzed to determine their internal consistency. Alpha coefficients ranged from .74 to .94. All scales were therefore judged reliable for further analysis.

Respondents were asked to rank order the nine morale scales in order of their need for improvement at UH-Manoa. "1" indicates the most need for improvement, and "9" indicates the least need for improvement. Overall, faculty members perceive the greatest need for improvement in leadership and the reward/evaluation system, and they perceive the least need for improvement in their students and their collegial relations.

Scale:	$\overline{X}$
Leadership	3.44
Reward/Evaluation system	3.72
Advocacy for Faculty	4.02
Professional Worklife	4.42
Support Services	4.73
Personal Issues	5.55
Faculty Governance	5.61
Students	6.24
Collegial Relations	6.41

Table 2

MEANS BY ITEM FOR TOTAL FACULTY RESPONDENTS

ITEM	MEAN	STANDARD DEVIATION	N
PROFESSIONAL WORKLIFE			
1. Undergraduate teaching load	3.44	1.17	613
2. Graduate teaching load	3.85	1.04	678
3. Committee load	2.89	1.02	887
4. Advising load	3.39	.94	765
5. Service to the university	3.43	.94	931
6. Service to the community	3.79	.92	909
7. Consulting opportunities	3.33	1.25	714
8. Support for professional travel	2.71	1.54	941
9. Availability of graduate assistants	2.40	1.39	759
10. Technician support	2.64	1.42	859
11. Clerical support	2.92	1.43	976
12. Access to institutional research funds	2.69	1.30	869
13. Access to extramural research funds	3.03	1.36	859
14. Access to project/program funds	2.85	1.33	841
15. Institutional research support	2.59	1.33	858
16. Program funding level	2.47	1.31	920
17. Administrative program support	2.63	1.31	918
18. Program staffing	2.67	1.22	892
19. Physical work environment	2.77	1.35	995
20. Parking	2.43	1.40	914
21. Reputation of UH-Manoa	2.92	1.08	988
REWARD/EVALUATION SYSTEM			
22. Institutional rewards for teaching	2.51	1.25	799
23. Institutional rewards for research	2.77	1.25	841
24. Institutional rewards for service	2.50	1.20	914
25. Feedback at contract renewal	2.94	1.18	724
26. Tenure process	2.69	1.14	736
27. Promotion process	2.67	1.16	807
28. Post-tenure review process	2.71	1.14	574
29. Graduate faculty status review	2.84	1.08	612

Table 2 (continued)

ITEM	MEAN	STANDARD DEVIATION	N
COLLEGIAL RELATIONS			
30. Relations with department chair or equivalent	3.78	1.29	992
31. Support for career from chair or equivalent	3.55	1.35	980
32. Social fit with department/unit	3.60	1.17	997
33. Intellectual fit with department/unit	3.64	1.19	1000
34. Collegial relations within department/unit	3.55	1.26	1004
35. Collegiality among UH-Manoa faculty	3.19	1.06	984
36. Access to colleagues off-campus	2.94	1.19	914
STUDENTS			
37. Enthusiasm of undergraduate students	3.23	1.30	758
38. Enthusiasm of graduate students	3.93	.99	864
39. Ability of undergraduate students	2.79	1.13	752
40. Ability of graduate students	3.52	1.06	860
41. Institutional support of undergraduates	2.73	1.07	713
42. Institutional support of graduate students	2.74	1.20	838
FACULTY GOVERNANCE			
Faculty input at the department or equivalent level:			
43. Academic/program decisions	3.49	1.26	940
44. Budget decisions	2.78	1.31	928
45. Personnel decisions	3.21	1.26	936
Faculty input at college or equivalent level:			
46. Academic/program decisions	2.67	1.18	874
47. Budget decisions	2.20	1.13	861
48. Personnel decisions	2.43	1.16	861
Faculty input at the university level:			
49. Academic/program decisions	2.26	1.13	848
50. Budget decisions	1.94	1.07	847
51. Personnel decisions	2.14	1.11	844
52. Protection of academic freedom	3.24	1.15	849
PERSONAL ISSUES			
53. Housing	2.47	1.35	826
54. Standard of living	2.43	1.25	937
55. Current salary	2.52	1.23	1002
56. Fringe benefits	2.77	1.20	974
57. Retirement benefits	2.56	1.22	954
58. Professional mobility	2.53	1.19	910

Table 2 (continued)

ITEM	MEAN	STANDARD DEVIATION	N
SUPPORT SERVICES			
59. Campus libraries	3.24	1.21	988
60. Office of Research Administration	2.83	1.07	852
61. Office of Faculty Development/Academic Support	2.90	1.09	784
62. Facilities (repair and maintenance)	2.22	1.10	947
63. Computing facilities	3.10	1.07	906
64. Duplicating/printing facilities	3.01	1.16	922
ADVOCACY FOR FACULTY			
65. Your Chair or equivalent	3.49	1.36	942
66. Your Dean/Director	2.97	1.39	920
67. Senior Central Administration	2.24	1.07	695
68. UH President/Chancellor	2.09	1.08	709
69. Board of Regents	1.90	.96	711
70. Legislature	1.84	.97	841
71. Governor	1.77	.93	804
72. Community	2.55	1.06	854
73. Manoa Faculty Senate	3.38	1.06	816
74. UH Professional Assembly (UHPA)	3.38	1.24	927
LEADERSHIP			
75. Your Chair or equivalent	3.45	1.39	980
76. Your Dean/Director	2.93	1.42	972
77. Senior Central Administration	2.26	1.04	761
78. UH President/Chancellor	2.25	1.11	787
79. Board of Regents	1.97	.96	801
80. Manoa Faculty Senate Executive Committee	3.09	1.03	768
81. UH Professional Assembly	3.10	1.22	931

Morale scales by demographic differences

Table 3 provides the means and standard deviations for female and male faculty members on each of the nine morale scales. T-tests indicate that two scales differ significantly by sex: students and leadership ($p < .01$). Female faculty indicate that their perceptions of the students and campus leadership are more positive than male faculty perceptions.

Table 4 provides the means and standard deviations on each of the nine morale scales by tenure status. There are significant differences on two scales: professional worklife and personal issues ($p < .01$). Tenured faculty indicate a more negative response to professional worklife, and non-tenured faculty indicate a more negative response to personal issues.

Analysis of variance was used to analyze the data by faculty classification and academic rank. Table 5 indicates that there are significant differences on six of the scales: professional worklife, students, personal issues, support services, advocacy for faculty and leadership ($p < .01$). Although no strong patterns emerge, it is worth noting that the means of the instructional faculty are consistently lower than that of the total faculty.

Similarly, Table 6 indicates that five of the scales differ significantly by academic rank: collegial relations, students, personal issues, advocacy for faculty and leadership ($p < .01$). Of these five, full professors indicate a more negative response than other academic ranks on all the scales except personal issues, which generates a more negative response from assistant professors and instructors.

Finally, Tables 7 and 8 provide the means on the morale scales by race/ethnicity and by locus of appointment. Due to the small numbers in some cells, no tests of significance were conducted.

Overall change in morale

One question was retained from the original survey in order to examine the general trend in faculty morale over the last ten years. Respondents were asked to indicate on a scale of "1" to "10" to what extent their morale has declined or improved since the time of the last survey (1992) or since they became a faculty member at UH-Manoa. "1" indicates declined morale, "5.5" is the midpoint or unchanged morale, and "10" indicates improved morale.

Year	1984	1985	1987	1990	1992	1994
Mean	3.2	3.8	4.6	4.7	4.6	4.3

FACULTY MORALE SCALE MEANS BY GENDER

Table 3

	PROF WORKLIFE	REWARD/ EVAL SYSTEM	COLLEGIAL RELATIONS	STUDENTS	FACULTY GOVERNANCE	PERSONAL ISSUES	SUPPORT SERVICES	ADVOCACY FOR FACULTY	LEADERSHIP
	$\overline{X}$ (SD)	$\overline{X}$ (SD)	$\overline{X}$ (SD)	$\overline{X}$ (SD)	$\overline{X}$ (SD)	$\overline{X}$ (SD)	$\overline{X}$ (SD)	$\overline{X}$ (SD)	$\overline{X}$ (SD)
TOTAL RESPONDENTS	2.95	2.71	3.48	3.17	2.64	2.55	2.89	2.57	2.73
FEMALE N=341	2.95 (.61)	2.70 (.66)	3.51 (.82)	3.30 (.63)	2.62 (.76)	2.57 (.86)	2.96 (.70)	2.60 (.58)	2.81 (.64)
MALE N=615	2.95 (.63)	2.71 (.69)	3.46 (.84)	3.10 (.70)	2.65 (.81)	2.54 (.93)	2.85 (.67)	2.55 (.59)	2.69 (.64)
P VALUE*	.914	.801	.405	.000	.546	.577	.017	.249	.005

*significance of t-ratio

Table 4

FACULTY MORALE SCALE MEANS BY TENURE STATUS

	PROF WORKLIFE	REWARD/ EVAL SYSTEM	COLLEGIAL RELATIONS	STUDENTS	FACULTY GOVERNANCE	PERSONAL ISSUES	SUPPORT SERVICES	ADVOCACY FOR FACULTY	LEADERSHIP
	$\bar{X}$ (SD)	$\bar{X}$ (SD)	$\bar{X}$ (SD)	$\bar{X}$ (SD)	$\bar{X}$ (SD)	$\bar{X}$ (SD)	$\bar{X}$ (SD)	$\bar{X}$ (SD)	$\bar{X}$ (SD)
TOTAL RESPONDENTS	2.95	2.71	3.48	3.17	2.64	2.55	2.89	2.57	2.73
TENURED N=504	2.87 (.61)	2.74 (.67)	3.42 (.82)	3.12 (.69)	2.63 (.30)	2.63 (.89)	2.84 (.68)	2.54 (.60)	2.69 (.66)
NON-TENURED N=453	3.04 (.63)	2.66 (.67)	3.53 (.85)	3.21 (.66)	2.64 (.79)	2.45 (.92)	2.93 (.69)	2.59 (.57)	2.77 (.63)
P VALUE*	.000	.062	.033	.059	.862	.002	.040	.200	.058

* significance of t-ratio

Table 5

FACULTY MORALE SCALE MEANS BY FACULTY CLASSIFICATION

	PROF WORKLIFE $\bar{X}$ (SD)	REWARD/ EVAL SYSTEM $\bar{X}$ (SD)	COLLEGIAL RELATIONS $\bar{X}$ (SD)	STUDENTS $\bar{X}$ (SD)	FACULTY GOVERNANCE $\bar{X}$ (SD)	PERSONAL ISSUES $\bar{X}$ (SD)	SUPPORT SERVICES $\bar{X}$ (SD)	ADVOCACY FOR FACULTY $\bar{X}$ (SD)	LEADERSHIP $\bar{X}$ (SD)
TOTAL RESPONDENTS	2.95	2.71	3.48	3.17	2.64	2.55	2.89	2.57	2.73
INSTRUCTOR N=604	2.83 (.62)	2.69 (.68)	3.42 (.83)	3.12 (.70)	2.62 (.76)	2.46 (.87)	2.79 (.69)	2.53 (.56)	2.69 (.62)
RESEARCHER N=121	3.06 (.63)	2.73 (.67)	3.51 (.86)	3.06 (.66)	2.59 (.82)	2.72 (.98)	3.05 (.64)	2.58 (.58)	2.72 (.66)
SPECIALIST N=144	3.15 (.64)	2.72 (.64)	3.59 (.85)	3.37 (.65)	2.73 (.89)	2.72 (.94)	3.13 (.67)	2.64 (.58)	2.86 (.70)
LIBRARIAN N=29	2.80 (.55)	2.93 (.53)	3.66 (.76)	3.39 (.64)	2.80 (.64)	2.46 (.74)	2.97 (.54)	2.95 (.77)	3.02 (.75)
AGENT N=29	3.01 (.59)	2.77 (.73)	3.46 (.80)	3.07 (.39)	2.63 (.83)	2.77 (.91)	2.86 (.71)	2.71 (.54)	2.66 (.59)
P VALUE*	.000	.439	.139	.000	.401	.001	.000	.001	.006

* significance of F-ratio

Table 6

FACULTY MORALE SCALE MEANS BY ACADEMIC RANK

	PROF WORKLIFE $\bar{X}$ (SD)	REWARD/ EVAL SYSTEM $\bar{X}$ (SD)	COLLEGIAL RELATIONS $\bar{X}$ (SD)	STUDENTS $\bar{X}$ (SD)	FACULTY GOVERNANCE $\bar{X}$ (SD)	PERSONAL ISSUES $\bar{X}$ (SD)	SUPPORT SERVICES $\bar{X}$ (SD)	ADVOCACY FOR FACULTY $\bar{X}$ (SD)	LEADERSHIP $\bar{X}$ (SD)
TOTAL RESPONDENTS	2.95	2.71	3.48	3.17	2.64	2.55	2.89	2.57	2.73
INSTRUCTOR N=56	3.09 (.61)	2.86 (.63)	3.76 (.80)	3.48 (.68)	2.86 (.73)	2.46 (.81)	3.10 (.69)	2.84 (.46)	3.02 (.54)
ASSISTANT N=259	2.96 (.61)	2.63 (.60)	3.52 (.80)	3.09 (.64)	2.59 (.70)	2.30 (.85)	2.86 (.70)	2.58 (.60)	2.74 (.62)
ASSOCIATE N=239	2.94 (.65)	2.71 (.75)	3.41 (.87)	3.19 (.66)	2.68 (.87)	2.52 (.95)	2.86 (.63)	2.53 (.59)	2.70 (.63)
FULL N=331	2.87 (.61)	2.75 (.66)	3.37 (.83)	3.08 (.72)	2.58 (.78)	2.73 (.89)	2.79 (.70)	2.51 (.60)	2.65 (.67)
P VALUE*	.052	.053	.004	.000	.049	.000	.016	.001	.001

* significance of F-ratio

Table 7

FACULTY MORALE SCALE MEANS BY RACE/ETHNICITY

	PROF WORKLIFE $\overline{X}$ (SD)	REWARD/ EVAL SYSTEM $\overline{X}$ (SD)	COLLEGIAL RELATIONS $\overline{X}$ (SD)	STUDENTS $\overline{X}$ (SD)	FACULTY GOVERNANCE $\overline{X}$ (SD)	PERSONAL ISSUES $\overline{X}$ (SD)	SUPPORT SERVICES $\overline{X}$ (SD)	ADVOCACY FOR FACULTY $\overline{X}$ (SD)	LEADERSHIP $\overline{X}$ (SD)
TOTAL RESPONDENTS	2.95	2.71	3.48	3.17	2.64	2.55	2.89	2.57	2.73
AFRIC-AMER N=2	2.49 (.56)	2.54 (.63)	3.86 (.81)	2.99 (.70)	2.31 (.57)	1.46 (.65)	2.64 (.03)	1.96 (1.22)	2.29 (1.21)
CAUCASION N=549	2.89 (.61)	2.67 (.63)	3.51 (.81)	3.10 (.67)	2.63 (.77)	2.44 (.90)	2.83 (.68)	2.52 (.58)	2.70 (.63)
CHINESE N=42	3.15 (.63)	2.88 (.67)	3.71 (.72)	3.15 (.72)	2.87 (.70)	2.89 (.83)	3.13 (.68)	2.83 (.58)	3.06 (.68)
FILIPINO N=14	3.44 (.72)	3.06 (.68)	4.02 (.75)	3.62 (.99)	3.10 (1.03)	2.75 (1.14)	3.18 (.67)	2.89 (.42)	3.09 (.46)
HAWAIIAN N=18	3.13 (.69)	2.57 (.65)	3.57 (.76)	3.36 (.89)	2.82 (.71)	2.46 (.81)	3.02 (.77)	2.82 (.73)	3.04 (.76)
HISPANIC N=7	2.82 (.65)	2.43 (.77)	2.97 (1.01)	3.07 (.55)	2.10 (.79)	2.63 (1.06)	2.24 (1.08)	2.56 (.45)	2.60 (.71)
JAPANESE N=93	3.18 (.61)	2.81 (.69)	3.61 (.81)	3.36 (.61)	2.71 (.76)	2.90 (.76)	3.10 (.63)	2.73 (.55)	2.82 (.61)
KOREAN N=5	3.01 (1.22)	2.83 (1.37)	3.53 (1.03)	3.47 (1.34)	3.02 (1.21)	2.93 (1.54)	2.87 (1.36)	2.44 (.61)	2.60 (.57)
NATIVE-AM N=4	2.92 (1.02)	2.35 (.82)	2.46 (1.04)	3.57 (1.22)	2.40 (1.77)	2.89 (1.65)	2.80 (.32)	1.76 (.57)	1.74 (.77)
SAMOAN N=0	—	—	—	—	—	—	—	—	—
OTHER N=24	3.03 (.58)	2.84 (.62)	3.25 (.94)	3.34 (.51)	2.75 (.75)	2.80 (.82)	3.22 (.63)	2.63 (.69)	2.86 (.73)

Table 8

FACULTY MORALE SCALE MEANS BY LOCUS OF APPOINTMENT

	PROF WORKLIFE	REWARD/ EVAL SYSTEM	COLLEGIAL RELATIONS	STUDENTS	FACULTY GOVERNANCE	PERSONAL ISSUES	SUPPORT SERVICES	ADVOCACY FOR FACULTY	LEADERSHIP
	$\bar{X}$	$\bar{X}$	$\bar{X}$	$\bar{X}$	$\bar{X}$	$\bar{X}$	$\bar{X}$	$\bar{X}$	$\bar{X}$
TOTAL RESPONDENTS	2.95	2.71	3.48	3.17	2.64	2.55	2.89	2.57	2.73
Arts&Hum N=75	2.78	2.68	3.25	3.03	2.45	2.32	2.75	2.33	2.54
LLL N=85	2.81	2.59	3.38	3.17	2.47	2.23	2.75	2.33	2.56
NaturalSci N=66	2.88	2.72	3.40	2.87	2.58	2.47	2.97	2.58	2.57
SocialSci N=66	2.69	2.61	3.36	2.82	2.65	2.28	2.69	2.46	2.65
BusinessAd N=31	2.80	2.70	3.39	3.23	2.71	2.64	2.82	2.60	2.64
CCECS N=9	3.35	3.04	3.45	3.74	3.38	3.25	3.01	2.77	2.90
Education N=109	3.10	2.77	3.84	3.47	2.91	2.53	2.92	2.68	2.93
Engineering N=25	3.18	2.84	3.34	3.22	2.64	2.56	2.91	2.69	2.79
Medicine N=81	3.10	2.69	3.42	3.35	2.64	2.79	2.80	2.62	2.78
Nursing N=26	2.82	2.82	3.59	3.40	2.88	2.55	2.86	2.88	3.02
PublicHealth N=15	2.84	2.40	3.20	3.10	2.08	2.71	3.02	2.44	2.39
SocialWork N=13	2.84	2.58	2.79	2.83	2.29	2.28	2.67	2.18	2.36
TropAg N=138	2.97	2.71	3.46	3.08	2.62	2.68	3.02	2.55	2.67

Table 8 (continued)

	PROF WORKLIFE	REWARD/ EVAL SYSTEM	COLLEGIAL RELATIONS	STUDENTS	FACULTY GOVERNANCE	PERSONAL ISSUES	SUPPORT SERVICES	ADVOCACY FOR FACULTY	LEADERSHIP
TOTAL RESPONDENTS	2.95	2.71	3.48	3.17	2.64	2.55	2.89	2.57	2.73
Architecture N=4	2.51	2.57	3.54	3.13	2.40	2.29	2.38	2.52	2.35
Law N=6	2.93	2.72	3.33	3.07	2.49	2.26	2.92	2.27	2.43
LibraryStudies N=2	3.23	3.06	4.57	3.52	2.92	3.33	3.17	3.06	3.18
LibraryService N=24	2.83	2.88	3.62	3.41	2.77	2.29	2.94	2.97	3.00
ResUnits/AA N=28	3.31	2.71	3.38	3.34	2.55	2.66	3.05	2.57	2.72
SOEST N=70	3.08	2.80	3.63	3.05	2.71	2.79	2.81	2.69	2.85
SNAPS N=14	3.42	2.82	3.74	3.20	2.62	2.57	3.22	2.67	2.94
StudentAffairs N=24	3.08	2.71	3.73	3.47	2.77	2.82	3.35	2.79	3.02
TIM N=6	2.85	3.11	3.29	3.62	2.74	2.73	3.13	2.81	3.16
Split Appt N=33	2.94	2.60	3.49	3.09	2.59	2.66	2.93	2.52	2.68

CONFIDENTIAL SURVEY OF UH-MANOA

FACULTY MORALE

The UH-Manoa Senate is conducting this confidential survey to assess faculty morale. We are interested in the current level of faculty morale and also in establishing baseline data to track the changes in faculty morale over time. Your responses will help the Senate in formulating recommendations to the administration.

Please indicate the extent to which each of the following factors contribute to your morale by circling the appropriate number. For example, a response of "1" indicates that this factor has negative impact on your morale. A response of "5" indicates that this factor has a positive impact on your morale. Circling NA indicates that the factor is not applicable to you personally.

Please rate the following factors in terms of their impact on your morale:

	Negative impact				Positive impact	
	1	2	3	4	5	NA
Professional worklife						
1. Undergraduate teaching load	1	2	3	4	5	NA
2. Graduate teaching load	1	2	3	4	5	NA
3. Committee load	1	2	3	4	5	NA
4. Advising load	1	2	3	4	5	NA
5. Service to the university	1	2	3	4	5	NA
6. Service to the community	1	2	3	4	5	NA
7. Consulting opportunities	1	2	3	4	5	NA
8. Support for professional travel	1	2	3	4	5	NA
9. Availability of graduate assistants	1	2	3	4	5	NA
10. Clerical support	1	2	3	4	5	NA
11. Access to institutional research funds	1	2	3	4	5	NA
12. Access to extramural research funds	1	2	3	4	5	NA
13. Institutional research support	1	2	3	4	5	NA
14. Physical work environment	1	2	3	4	5	NA
15. Parking	1	2	3	4	5	NA
16. Reputation of UH-Manoa	1	2	3	4	5	NA
Reward/evaluation system						
17. Institutional rewards for teaching	1	2	3	4	5	NA
18. Institutional rewards for research	1	2	3	4	5	NA
19. Institutional rewards for service	1	2	3	4	5	NA
20. Feedback at contract renewal	1	2	3	4	5	NA
21. Tenure process	1	2	3	4	5	NA
22. Promotion process	1	2	3	4	5	NA
23. Post-tenure review process	1	2	3	4	5	NA

Please rate the following factors in terms of their impact on your morale:

	Negative impact				Positive impact	
Collegial relations						
24. Relations with department chair	1	2	3	4	5	NA
25. Support for career from chair	1	2	3	4	5	NA
26. Social fit with department	1	2	3	4	5	NA
27. Intellectual fit with department	1	2	3	4	5	NA
28. Collegial relations within department	1	2	3	4	5	NA
29. Collegiality among UH-Manoa faculty	1	2	3	4	5	NA
Students						
30. Enthusiasm of undergraduate students	1	2	3	4	5	NA
31. Enthusiasm of graduate students	1	2	3	4	5	NA
32. Ability of undergraduate students	1	2	3	4	5	NA
33. Ability of graduate students	1	2	3	4	5	NA
34. Institutional support of undergraduates	1	2	3	4	5	NA
35. Institutional support of graduate students	1	2	3	4	5	NA
Faculty Governance						
Faculty input in department level:						
36.•academic decisions	1	2	3	4	5	NA
37.•budget decisions	1	2	3	4	5	NA
38.•personnel decisions	1	2	3	4	5	NA
Faculty input in college/unit level:						
39.•academic decisions	1	2	3	4	5	NA
40.•budget decisions	1	2	3	4	5	NA
41.•personnel decisions	1	2	3	4	5	NA
Faculty input in university level:						
42.•academic decisions	1	2	3	4	5	NA
43.•budget decisions	1	2	3	4	5	NA
44.•personnel decisions	1	2	3	4	5	NA
45. Protection of academic freedom	1	2	3	4	5	NA
Personal Factors						
46. Housing	1	2	3	4	5	NA
47. Standard of living	1	2	3	4	5	NA
48. Current salary	1	2	3	4	5	NA
49. Fringe benefits	1	2	3	4	5	NA
50. Retirement benefits	1	2	3	4	5	NA
51. Professional mobility	1	2	3	4	5	NA

Please take a moment to review the factors 1-51 listed above, and
•List three of these factors (or others) that have the most <u>negative</u> impact on your morale.
1._____ 2._____ 3._____
Please take a moment to review the factors 1-51 listed above, and
•List three of these factors (or others) that have the most <u>positive</u> impact on your morale.
1._____ 2._____ 3._____

Please rate the following factors in terms of their impact on <u>your ability to function effectively</u>:

	Negative impact				Positive impact	
52. Hamilton Library	1	2	3	4	5	NA
53. Office of Research Administration	1	2	3	4	5	NA
54. Office of Faculty Dev/Academic Support	1	2	3	4	5	NA
55. Facilities (repair & maintenance)	1	2	3	4	5	NA
56. Computing facilities	1	2	3	4	5	NA

Please rate the way you view the <u>advocacy for UH-Manoa faculty by</u>:

	Weak				Strong	
57. Your Chair	1	2	3	4	5	NA
58. Your Dean/Director	1	2	3	4	5	NA
59. Central Administration	1	2	3	4	5	NA
60. UH President	1	2	3	4	5	NA
61. Board of Regents	1	2	3	4	5	NA
62. Legislature	1	2	3	4	5	NA
63. Governor	1	2	3	4	5	NA
64. Community	1	2	3	4	5	NA
65. Manoa Faculty Senate	1	2	3	4	5	NA
66. UH Professional Assembly (UHPA)	1	2	3	4	5	NA

Please rate the <u>confidence you have in the leadership exhibited by</u>:

	Low confidence				High confidence	
67. Your Chair	1	2	3	4	5	NA
68. Your Dean/Director	1	2	3	4	5	NA
69. Central Administration	1	2	3	4	5	NA
70. UH President	1	2	3	4	5	NA
71. Board of Regents	1	2	3	4	5	NA
72. Manoa Faculty Senate Exec. Committee	1	2	3	4	5	NA
73. UH Professional Assembly (UHPA)	1	2	3	4	5	NA

Demographic Information

Lastly (you are almost finished!), please answer the following items so that we may make a more informed interpretation of the data.

Faculty classification: How is your appointment categorized?

Instructional (I, I-R, I-S, I-M, J)   _____
Researcher (R)   _____
Specialist (S)   _____
Librarian (B)   _____
Agent ( )   _____
Other   _____
Split appointment (please specify)   _____

Number of years on Manoa Faculty?   _____
Age (please check one)   _____ 22-35   _____ 36-45
    _____ 46-55   _____ 56-65
    _____ 65+

Gender   _____ Female   _____ Male

Race/Ethnicity (please indicate group with which you most closely identify):
_____

I have (check one)   _____ a 9-month appointment.
                          _____ an 11-month appointment.

Locus of appointment (if split check more than one):
College of Arts & Sciences:
    Arts & Humanities.................................   _____
    Languages, Linguistics, & Literature............   _____
    Natural Sciences....................................   _____
    Social Sciences.....................................   _____
College of Business Administration......................   _____
College of Continuing Education & Community Service   _____
College of Education..   _____
College of Engineering.....................................   _____
College of Health Sciences & Social Welfare:
    School of Medicine................................   _____
    School of Nursing.................................   _____
    School of Public Health...........................   _____
    School of Social Work.............................   _____
College of Tropical Agriculture & Human Resources....   _____
School of Architecture......................................   _____
School of Law..   _____
School of Library Studies.................................   _____
Library Services..   _____
Organized Research Units & Academic Affairs...........   _____
SOEST...   _____
SHAPS..   _____
Student Affairs..   _____
Travel Industry Management.............................   _____

_____

Feel free to add any other comments.

Please return this survey in the enclosed envelope to:
Dr. Linda K. Johnsrud, Chair
Manoa Faculty Senate
Bachman Annex 9-E

THANK YOU VERY MUCH FOR YOUR TIME AND EFFORT.

YOUR PARTICIPATION IS GREATLY APPRECIATED.

Chapter 10

From Data to Action

The two preceding case studies provide actual examples of morale assessments conducted to inform those who have the power to address morale issues. The results of morale assessments are of little value unless they are used to enhance the quality of work life for administrative staff and faculty. Results need to be translated into concrete recommendations; the results and recommendations need to be disseminated; and recommendations need to be translated into policy and program initiatives.

From Results to Recommendations

The process used to formulate priorities and recommendations in the administrator case study presented in Chapter 8 was similar to the qualitative research method of triangulation; that is, findings were checked against one another to establish congruence and the contribution of each set of findings to the whole. For example, the rank-ordering of each work-related issue indicated which issues were most important to administrative staff; the factors generated from the items and used in the regression indicated which of the factors actually predicted high and low morale; and finally, the qualitative comments provided a check on the positive and negative effect of each of the issues. Working from one set of findings to another, a pattern becomes apparent of priorities that represents a composite of what is important to morale.

Once the priorities are determined, it is a matter of addressing each priority relative to its effect. Those issues that are related to *high* morale (for example, support for career development) need to be affirmed; supervisors need to be reinforced to provide career training and support for their staff members. Those issues that are related to *low* morale (for example, discrimination) need to be addressed; supervisors need to guard against bias and the perception of bias by being scrupulously fair in decisions regarding personnel. The data indicate what is most important as well as whether it has a negative or positive effect on morale. Both pieces of information are necessary to generate appropriate recommendations.

Who Generates Recommendations?

It could be argued, and has been, that the researcher should generate and interpret the data, and leave to others the movement from results to recommendations for action. Some researchers feel that issues of policy and practice are the province of others and that they should remain above "application." Researchers are often in the best position to evaluate the relative importance of the issues based on the data. In fact, findings are rarely reported without making choices about priorities. The very act of generating a final report requires decisions about the presentation of the findings that gives prominence to some findings and lessens the significance of others.

Whether researchers go the next step and actually make recommendations depends on their ability to do so. Recommendations need to be not only grounded in the data, but also realistic. Recommendations that are all high-cost or "pie-in-the-sky" will be dismissed. If those who conducted the assessment are not sufficiently savvy to the realities and the politics of the campus, they need to turn to those who are. Members of the advisory board can play an important role in reviewing recommendations to be sure they are balanced. Recommendations need to reflect the actual concerns expressed in the findings, as well as demonstrate a sense of priorities that senior administrators can evaluate and, hopefully, implement.

Of the two cases presented in Chapters 8 and 9, the administrative staff case included recommendations; the other, the faculty case, did not. The reasons for the difference lie in the history and what preceded each assessment. In the case of the administrative staff assessment, there had never been a comparable effort. This survey was the first time that the morale of this group had been assessed and the project attracted quite a bit of attention. Many of the comments written on the instruments themselves indicated how grateful the members of the administrative staff were for the attention and how eager they were to learn the results. Nonetheless, many were also cynical as to whether "anything would come of the effort." These sentiments, coupled with the willingness of the leadership of the human resource office to have recommendations generated, led to the production of the list of recommendations presented in the technical report.

In the case of the faculty assessment (Chapter 9), there was no precedent for including recommendations. A morale survey had been conducted for several years by the Senate and the results had always been presented without comment. This procedure seemed to serve faculty interests. For example, in the faculty morale assessment, it was clear that faculty felt quite positive about their students, and quite negative about leadership and the system of rewards and evaluation. This information was used to advantage by the Chair of the Faculty Senate who emphasized publicly how this finding demonstrated that, contrary to popular belief, students, both undergraduate and graduate, are important to faculty. There is power in the positive nature of this finding. At the same time, the Senate initiated two task forces: one to review the tenure and promotion guidelines and another to explore the system of evaluating senior administrators, especially deans, vice presidents, and presidents.

This use of data is clearly political and proactive. The Faculty Senate did not wait for members of the administration to react to recommendations. Rather, they took the initiative to address the concerns themselves. Armed with the relevant data, they took on issues that will undoubtedly be controversial and justified their actions as "mandated by the faculty."

Given the faculty's role in governance of the institution and authority over their own affairs, they are more able to take this approach than midlevel administrators are. Often midlevel administrators are not represented by an organized group (unless they are part of a collective bargaining unit) and have little control over the quality of their work lives. For midlevel administrators, it is all the more important for them to "work through channels" and have a set of concrete recommendations based on credible data to present to the senior administration.

Dissemination of the Findings and the Recommendations

A major reason for disseminating the final reports broadly is to call attention to them. The more attention they receive, the less likely they are to be ignored by those with the authority to attend to the issues. Broad dissemination of the results of the assessment also is important to respondents. They want to know that the time they spent on the survey was not wasted and that their responses received attention. Any sense that the results of the assessment were "buried" will create animosity and distrust for the entire process. Moreover, respondents and nonrespondents are curious; they will be eager to see if their perceptions are similar to those of their colleagues. In fact, the very knowledge that others feel the same way can serve to lessen the personalization of what is often a structural issue. For example, one member of the APT staff wrote a personal letter indicating her appreciation of the survey effort and added that she had been disgruntled with her position relative to a particular faculty member until she realized that her situation was not unique. As she remarked, "I can handle it better knowing that it is not just me; it is a function of the system."

Dissemination of both reports included here occurred in a formal manner. A draft of the APT technical report was shared with the sponsors of the study, the Director of EEO/Affirmative Action and the System Director of Human Resources, as a courtesy. They responded positively. The final technical report was transmitted to the Office of Human Resources as the primary sponsor of the study. The director then sent it on to the vice president of administration, who in turn transmitted it to the president of the university. From there it was made public and distributed to the University Executive Council, which includes the senior officers of all the campuses as well as system-wide officers.

Subsequently the Office of Human Resources asked the researchers to make a keynote presentation regarding the findings of the study at a system-wide meeting of administrative and personnel officers. Copies of the executive summary were distributed; and it was announced that copies of the entire technical report were available in the main library of each of the 10 campuses. Finally, the system-wide weekly newspaper, *Ku Lama*, which goes to every member of the university faculty and staff, carried an article reporting the results of the study.

The process of dissemination differed for the faculty morale assessment because it was sponsored by the University of Hawaii at Manoa Faculty Senate;

thus, the final report was disseminated by the Senate Executive Committee. A copy was mailed to every senator and the findings presented at a senate meeting. Copies also were sent to the president and chancellor, the vice chancellor for academic affairs, the deans and directors, and other academic administrators. The student newspaper, *Ka Leo,* featured the findings in a front-page article.

From Recommendations to Action

Once disseminated, it is important to maintain interest and commitment to the outcomes of the morale assessment. Advisory board members can be of help if they are willing to sponsor open forums or brown bag luncheons to discuss the results. They also can make presentations to groups that can apply pressure or play a direct role in the implementation of the recommendations. For example, union boards, senates, faculty caucuses, and commissions on women and/or diversity can all apply pressure to senior administrators to enhance the quality of work life among faculty and staff. The more people talk about the issues of concern, the more likely there is to be action.

In Chapter 3 the importance of securing the support of key campus leaders was emphasized. It is at the point of implementation that support becomes crucial. Human resource officers and senior administrative officers are in key positions to exercise leadership regarding the work climate on campus. Presidents and other campus leaders who address issues of morale in their speeches can make a difference. When presidents take up the call for building morale and improving the conditions under which people work, their staffs will listen and are more likely to take positive steps.

A strength of the morale assessment process described here is that it generates sound quantitative data. Quantitative data carry the power of numbers. Specific statements can be made: There is a significant and positive relationship between the support midlevel administrators receive for their career development and their morale ($p < .01$); The most demoralizing personal issues for faculty are their inability to secure affordable housing and their standard of living (means of 2.43 and 2.47, respectively).

From these two statements, recommendations can be developed. If the data support the importance of career development to midlevel administrators, then human resource officers might respond with seminars and workshops designed to assist with career planning. The opportunities for mobility could be identified and, where appropriate, job ladders for advancement could be created or clarified so the options are evident. Mentoring or career coaching programs could be created to provide personal advice and support for developing one's career.

Similarly, the second finding suggests that if recruiting and retaining faculty are priorities of the institution, then certain personal issues, especially housing and the standard of living, should be addressed. More new and/or young faculty are disillusioned by the lack of affordable housing than any other single issue. Although this item has a potentially high cost, plans to financially assist faculty in purchasing homes can be explored. Some means, such as the institution serving as cosigner, may be used to reduce the down-payments required of faculty or to allow them to secure a lower interest rate. In the short run, a faculty housing office could be created that serves as a clearinghouse for long-term and short-term rentals as well as homes for purchase. Listings could be solicited from faculty and staff, alumni and supporters of the university interested in helping faculty find appropriate housing. Once increasing morale becomes a priority, the options to meet identified concerns are limited only by the creativity of those leading the effort.

Low-Cost and No-Cost Responses to Administrative Staff Morale Issues

Some administrators will argue there is no such thing as a no-cost response. And in fact, given that the scarcest resource is often time, this argument may well be true. Low cost and no-cost means no influx of new dollars is required. The conscious decision to attend to the quality of work life of staff and faculty requires more of an attitude change or a shift in priorities than in increased dollars. The results of the midlevel administrator study demonstrated the relative importance of salary. Although salary was considered very important by a significant number of respondents, salary (as included in the factor working conditions) was not a significant predictor of morale. Money is important to people; equity in the allocation of monies is even more important; and other work related issues are even more important to their morale. For example, the following recommendations were made based on the findings of the midlevel administrator study. Each one can be addressed to at least some degree at very little new cost to the institution.

CAREER MOBILITY. Clarify career paths that provide the means for advancement of APTs. Feeling stagnant in a position with little expectation of mobility is a significant contributor to low morale.

In too many organizations, employees are afraid to talk about their interest in career mobility because they fear supervisors will consider them disloyal or uncommitted. Good workers want to be challenged; they want to develop their skills and they often want to move through the system. It is short sighted to think that ignoring their interest in career advancement is going to keep them in their current jobs. If the institution is proactive about career development, the individual may not stay in his or her current position or even in a particular unit but they are more likely to remain committed to the institution.

It is the reality of most organizational structures that there are increasingly fewer positions as one moves up the pyramid-like hierarchy. Nonetheless, colleges and universities are complex organizations; there are numerous institutes, centers, and affiliated programs besides the typical array of positions in academic, student, external, and business affairs. Midlevel administrators can build challenging careers moving within a given institution, but often they cannot readily see the opportunities. Human resource offices can generate career histories on current employees and trace the positions through which they moved to get where they are. Or they can analyze the skills and background required for various positions and model sequences of jobs that require increasing skills and experience. This information must then be made available to mid- and entry-level administrators who can use it in their personal career planning.

On an individual basis, employees can be encouraged to identify positions of interest and arrange for job exchanges, short-term internships, or internal sabbaticals that are intended to enhance the skills and experience of the individual—to the benefit of the institution. Such experiences can be coordinated by the human resource offices or through personal connections. Establishing a voluntary mentoring or coaching program in which those who have moved successfully within the institution help newcomers makes such opportunities widely available. Not everyone will avail themselves, but those who do will gain, the institution will gain, and the very fact that such opportunities exist and are supported will mean that far fewer people will feel "stuck."

RECOGNITION. Establish ways of recognizing the contributions of APTs to their work units and to the university as a whole. Supervisors need to express appreciation for a job well done and recognition for the quality of the effort expended.

Showing appreciation sounds so simple, it is hard to believe that it is ever an issue, but supervisors who are busy and working hard do not often think to take the time to stop and express their appreciation of those working with or for them. There are all sorts of low-cost perks that can be used such as: honoring an employee of the month or an entire unit of the month, displaying plaques and pictures prominently, featuring high achievers in newsletters, designating special parking for a period of time, or giving luncheons and receptions in honor of a job well done. Colleges and universities have been slow to make such efforts and some will not see it as in keeping with their ethos. Such perks tend to be individualistic and competitive and many institutions are trying to reinforce more collaborative efforts and a stronger sense of community. If public acknowledgments do not seem appropriate to the culture of the campus, then senior administrators and supervisors need to show their appreciation in small, personal ways. Receiving a handwritten note of recognition and appreciation for a special effort or a particular accomplishment feels great and is surprisingly rare.

CLASSIFICATION/COMPENSATION SYSTEM. Review the job classification and compensation system to ensure that it is based on performance and workload distribution. Many APTs want performance appraisals that reward performance based on merit. One specific issue that causes tension is the lack of parity with those in other classifications performing essentially the same tasks.

In this case, the morale assessment uncovered a source of real frustration for many APTs. The system of classifying their jobs and determining the worth of the job to the institution was long overdue for a review. This frustration might have been unique to this system but, in general, all job classifications systems need periodic review. New jobs are added, old ones deleted, exceptions are made, and eventually the system becomes less than systematic. Moreover, the APTs as a group were not receiving performance appraisals. In this case, it was an issue that had to be handled through collective bargaining, but clearly the data suggest that it was a matter of sufficient concern to be addressed.

SKILL DEVELOPMENT. Foster the development of APT management and leadership skills, including supervisory and management techniques, personnel policies, and legal guidelines that relate to their responsibilities.

Skill development does not necessarily mean career mobility. Some individuals simply want to enhance their performance in the job they have; others want to build skills and abilities to move up. In either case, the institution is well served to provide the means for their midlevel administrators to develop their talents. Colleges and universities have a wealth of resources for advanced education and training on their campuses. Many institutions provide tuition waivers but not all individuals benefit. Often policies are unevenly applied. Some supervisors will not allow employees to use work hours for class; others require that the education must be related to the job they are currently holding. Every effort should be made to support education and training for employees, and whatever the policies that are agreed on should be applied uniformly. Once again, the perception of bias or discrimination is demoralizing.

Also, training does not need to entail college-level courses. Seminars and workshops addressing topics such as supervisory skills; leadership skills; time management; use of technology; the Internet, and e-mail; personnel policies, and legalities pertinent to higher education are important to midlevel administrators' success in their jobs. Such efforts are too often eliminated during tough times—when they are most needed. When budgets are tight, institutions need to turn to internal resources and find creative ways to lessen the costs. It is counterproductive to eliminate staff training and development.

RED TAPE. *Identify and eliminate bureaucratic red tape and/or regulations that create unnecessary work. Incentives could be instituted to find creative ways to streamline work and save time and money.*

An efficiency committee can be initiated that awards prizes to employees for suggestions that cut down on red tape, that eliminate unnecessary forms or procedures, or that simply increase the efficiency of a unit or the university. A column could be run in a faculty and staff newsletter that encourages employees to clip it out and send in their tips to increase efficiency.

TEAM BUILDING. *Provide workshops specifically designed to enhance team building and communication between APTs, their supervisors, and coworkers.*

Entire units can get into a funk for all sorts of reasons (e.g., new leadership, no new leadership, high turnover, no turnover, low performance, uneven performance, ill-defined expectations, external pressure, etc.). When a unit has low morale, it may require external intervention. A day-long workshop, a retreat, or a series of sessions may be needed to help the unit regroup, reaffirm its goals, and generate new ways of working together that raise morale and performance.

Employees' trust of their supervisors is important to their morale. There are conflicting views on the degree of trust that should be proffered to staff members. Some would argue that trust must be earned; others maintain that it is best to trust until that trust is violated. Obviously, these views represent different perspectives on human nature. It is unlikely that the perspective of a particular supervisor is going to be changed, but it is important for him or her to realize the power of his or her attitudes or actions on departmental team building. When individuals are chosen for supervisory positions, they ought to have the ability or be trained in ways to build rapport, motivate their staff, communicate, build a cohesive team, and establish a positive work environment. If they cannot or do not do so, they need to receive help to develop these skills or they need to be relieved of their positions.

Low-Cost and No-Cost Responses to Faculty Morale Issues

Although there were no recommendations disseminated with the technical report in the case study of faculty (Chapter 9), recommendations can easily be developed based on the findings of the study. As noted earlier, faculty play a more significant role in their own affairs than do midlevel administrators because they have a formal role in governance. Therefore, they can respond to certain morale issues, such as initiatives regarding the faculty reward and evaluation system as well as the evaluation of senior administrators. The senior administration can, however, take an equally proactive response to faculty issues that fall within the administrative domain. The following are recommendations that could be addressed directly by senior administrators to enhance the morale of faculty. Examples of low cost and no-cost responses are emphasized.

LEADERSHIP. *The lack of confidence in the leadership of the institution is a major morale issue that demands a creative and sensitive response.*

It may be the case that faculty are rarely enamored with the leadership of their institution; this situation does not mean that the issue should be ignored. An important finding in these data is that the confidence the faculty have in their leaders decreases with the distance the leaders are from the faculty (i.e., they have the most confidence in their chairs, less in their deans, even less in vice presidents and presidents, etc.). It is also apparent that faculty perceive a decreasing strength of advocacy from leaders distant from them.

These findings suggest that faculty feel more trust for those they know better and presumably communicate with more frequently. This finding may serve to alert senior administrators to the need for increased communication and interaction with all members of the campus community. Presidents need to be visible on their campuses; so do deans. On the presidential level, increased communication may include a monthly presidential newsletter or a weekly column in a faculty and staff bulletin. Vice presidents of academic affairs, deans, and directors can make greater efforts to communicate so their faculty and staff feel they know "what is going on." Admittedly, there is a limit to the ability of senior administrators to interact individually with great numbers of faculty or staff, but typically more can be done than is being done. Senior administrators can initiate more social gatherings, invited luncheons with members of particular units or representatives to senates, faculty and staff dining areas or clubs that bring administrators (senior and midlevel) and faculty together, and no-host breakfasts or cocktail parties that create a sense of campus community.

Confidence in leadership also can be enhanced with increased understanding of the pressures confronting campus leaders. The more faculty know and understand the goals, values, and priorities of senior administrators, the more they are likely to trust their leadership. Leaders need to lessen the ambiguity and clarify their direction. Faculty may not agree with the direction but they would rather be in a position to challenge and debate than to be kept in the dark.

REWARD AND EVALUATION SYSTEM. *The anxiety expressed by all faculty regarding tenure and promotion is not unique to this campus but is an issue that contributes to alienation and frustration. Unclear and/or shifting expectations seem to be the primary source of the problem.*

An overriding issue of concern on many campuses is the appropriate balance between teaching, research, and service. Faculty need to address this issue and arrive at standards in keeping with the ethos and mission of their institution. Many faculty believe that teaching and service need to be emphasized to a far greater extent than they are currently. To shift the priorities of faculty, the system of rewards and evaluation must be addressed.

Within an up-to-date institutional framework, departments should be required to update and clarify their tenure and promotion criteria. An explicit statement of expectations should be included in the letter of appointment issued to new tenure-track faculty. All department chairs and/or department personnel committee chairs should be trained to provide timely, thorough, and constructive performance reviews to untenured faculty. Annual reviews ought to explicitly address progress toward tenure; that is, the individual's progress should be measured against the departmental criteria and concrete recommendations made for a positive decision.

Chairs and departmental personnel committees should carefully monitor the progress of untenured faculty and, when appropriate, encourage them to pursue tenure early. Early tenure can serve to retain faculty. The granting of tenure demonstrates departmental and institutional commitment to faculty and relieves the pervading sense of anxiety experienced by many untenured faculty.

The teaching, advising, and service load of faculty should be monitored. Departments should be required to support the efforts of faculty to meet tenure and promotion criteria by allocating workload appropriately. The tenure and promotion dossier requirements should be streamlined. Concise, factual presentation should be encouraged and excessive self-promotion discouraged.

Rewards for excellence in teaching and research should be meaningful. Searching about for those who have not received "theirs" yet, makes a mockery of the honor. Recognition for these awards also might include the allocation of a graduate assistant for the following year, not only to reward the faculty member, but also to provide the students with an exemplary model for teaching and/or research.

INSTITUTIONAL SUPPORT. Although salary is the most frequently cited economic need by all faculty, other forms of support or compensation also are needed. The equitable distribution of resources is vital to morale.

Salary is important. Faculty have long endured low pay relative to their educational attainments. During tough times, modest increases in salary should remain a priority. Most important, if salaries are frozen, they should be frozen across the board, including the salaries of senior administrative officers.

Similarly, no matter what the resource—graduate assistants, parking, monies for professional travel, clerical support, or computer software—it is exceedingly important for faculty to believe that the available resources are being distributed fairly and/or according to some equitable criteria. Departments and schools should be charged to review their policies for distributing such resources to ensure that all faculty members are receiving equitable and timely support. Graduate assistants, whether teaching or research, should be available on a rotating basis to those faculty who show the most genuine need. Increasing the availability of graduate assistants also is a relatively low-cost means of supporting faculty research and teaching. Deans and chairs should be held responsible for ensuring that faculty at all ranks receive support and assistance.

Working conditions can be another source of frustration. Many campuses cut repair and maintenance budgets during tough times. Although this a short-term solution to a budget shortfall and one that often comes back to haunt administrators, if repair and maintenance is being curtailed, faculty should be made well aware of the decision and its consequences.

FACULTY GOVERNANCE/DEPARTMENTAL RELATIONS. The primary locus of faculty governance is at the department level. Although faculty governance per se did not have a negative effect on faculty in this study, relations between the department chair and faculty were viewed as very important to morale.

Relations existing between the chair and faculty members and within the department as a whole are crucial to the morale of faculty. One of the primary roles of the department chair should be to build and nurture a positive collegial climate in the department for all faculty. To accomplish this objective, the selection of chairs should be monitored carefully and ongoing training instituted. Training should include attention to issues of professional work climate, professional development and academic support, evaluation, sexual harassment, and affirmative action.

Department chairs also should be trained to recognize and confront inappropriate conduct. Chairs are in key positions to recognize and eliminate discrimination at the departmental level. Women and minorities are often isolated in departments, and as a result, depend on the awareness of the chair to ensure a positive working environment conducive to their retention and advancement.

Untenured faculty often feel the most left out of the processes of governance and most vulnerable to the decisions made. Junior faculty need the support and guidance of senior faculty. Mentoring programs, for all new junior faculty, should be supported and efforts made to reward senior faculty members for the time spent working with their less experienced colleagues. Collaborative research proposals that link senior and junior faculty or junior faculty with one another can be encouraged by giving joint proposals priority in internal funding competitions.

Budget decisions are the governance issue that is most frustrating to faculty. No matter what level—department, school, or institution—budget decisions, and the criteria for them, are too often kept quiet. Soliciting input from faculty in a timely manner regarding academic program priorities could do much to enhance morale. Faculty recognize that difficult choices must be made but they most resent being left out of the decision-making process.

COLLEGIAL RELATIONS: Positive relationships between colleagues contribute to positive morale. Senior administrators need to support efforts to build collegiality and maintain community.

Much can be done to build and support the positive interaction among faculty that is important to their morale. A faculty club is a first step. There are a variety of models, from noon dining only to full-scale hotels, but the ideal is to find a self-sustaining enterprise that will serve as a center for faculty gatherings. The size and layout of most campuses are not conducive to building relationships among faculty. New faculty, particularly ethnic and racial minorities and women, are isolated in most departments. A common meeting place would relieve the intellectual and social isolation as well as serve to create larger arenas than departments for faculty to interact.

Deliberate steps can be taken to enhance the social and intellectual interaction within the departments and schools. For example, faculty colloquia designed to challenge thinking, invigorate participants, and improve the sense of academic collegiality can be fostered. Colloquia and other collaborative projects (teaching as well as research) might lessen the gap between junior and senior faculty—bridging the differences in training and research orientation that contribute to the sense of isolation for many faculty.

The recommendations listed here are meant to enhance and maintain the morale of faculty. Most of the recommendations are low-cost items, but they require commitment from those in positions of responsibility as well as the interest of the department as a whole in addressing the quality of work life of faculty. Efforts such as those outlined will demonstrate institutional and departmental commitment to the career progress and well-being of faculty.

Low-cost and no-cost responses to those issues that diminish or enhance the morale of both faculty and midlevel administrators must be considered within the campus context. Once the data are analyzed, it may be best to hold some brainstorming sessions with the advisory board to generate ideas in keeping with the realities and culture of the campus. The key is to begin with the findings, examine the priorities expressed by the respondents, and then create ways to address those priorities. It is equally important to think about what enhances morale as it is to think about what diminishes morale. Positive, proactive actions are needed.

Chapter 11

Conclusion

The assessments and recommendations for raising morale presented in this book address the quality of work life of midlevel administrators and faculty. The assumptions are that enhancing the quality of work life will in turn enhance morale, and that morale is important to the quality and vitality of the academic enterprise. Quality of work life is, however, an internal matter. The current major threats to morale are reduced resources and restructuring, loss of credibility with the public, and increased internal conflict. By addressing quality of work life, there will be some who will charge that the deckchairs are being rearranged on the *Titanic*. And for those who have lost or will lose their jobs, concern about career ladders or the fair distribution of graduate assistants is superfluous at best.

Nonetheless, the issue of the morale of midlevel administrators and faculty is important and institutions can only address work-life morale by examining work-life issues. Beyond that, however, many of the work-life issues that emerged from the review of the literature and the case studies regarding staff and faculty are relevant to the issues of reduced resources, public disaffection, and internal conflict. Although these threats to the vitality of higher education are essentially out of the control of administrators and academics, attending to the quality of work life may be one means of not only coping, but also beginning to address the issues compounding our current malaise.

Reduced Resources and Restructuring

The most demoralizing aspect of the fiscal constraints plaguing higher education is that they do not appear to be short term. The golden days of the 1960s seem far removed from our current experience. There has been a considerable period of time in which many institutions had more than ample budgets; programs and personnel proliferated; problems were addressed with new staff; and no program, needed or not, was eliminated. The contrast with today's reality is overwhelming. There can, however, be a positive side to downsizing: the enhanced quality that comes from reexamining what is central to the mission of the institution and taking a hard look at programs and staffing to determine what may be redundant, outdated, or peripheral. There is much to be gained by identifying the priorities of an institution and consolidating the resources to enable the institution to meet those priorities.

Institutions can emerge from retrenchment with stronger and higher quality, albeit fewer, programs. That is the good news. How they accomplish this end and how they treat their staff and faculty in the process will determine the degree of bad news. Returning to the two morale assessments presented in Chapters 8 and 9, two key findings are relevant: the need for timely and honest communication, and the involvement of staff and faculty in decisions that will affect them. Staff and faculty want to know that everything is being done that can be done to protect their programs and positions from unnecessary or arbitrary cuts. Senior administrators need to let them know they are defending the institution against budget cuts and promoting the institution's contributions to the public good. Rumors are generated from the fear of the unknown. Only timely and honest communication will prevent rumors from further undermining morale.

If there is no policy or precedent for handling retrenchment, senior administrators should meet with their staff and faculty to hammer out a process for making difficult decisions. The criteria and priorities for cuts should be debated by the appropriate groups. For example, faculty within its representative body should address the issue of academic priorities. Faculty can make recommendations regarding the issue of across-the-board or selective cuts that eliminate programs. They also can set priorities regarding undergraduate education, graduate program and research areas, and academic support such as the libraries and academic computing facilities. Although midlevel administrators typically do not have a representative body, they should be called together within their respective units (i.e., student affairs, business affairs, external affairs, and academic affairs) to solicit their advice regarding program priorities. They, too, should be given a voice in the decision regarding across-the-board or selective cuts.

Both groups should be encouraged to identify all the cost-saving measures they can and to find new ways of delivering services for less cost. Technological advances can be brought to bear within administration and instruction. As Sidney Harman, board member of the Public Agenda for the California Education Policy Center, pointed out: higher education cannot expect the state to bail them out nor can it simply raise fees, cut enrollments or lower quality. Rather "higher education must be part of its own solution."[1]

Ultimately, on most campuses it is the senior administrators who will make the final decisions about restructuring, program consolidations, and, if need be, program elimination. Staff and faculty should have the opportunity to advise, but they should not be put in a position of making decisions about their own and their colleagues' jobs—that is what senior administrators are paid to do. If there is a collective bargaining contract, procedures affecting employment will be explicit. One omission in most contracts, however, is the relative priority of administrative cuts and instructional cuts.[2] A wise administration will give a good deal of thought to the balance between—and the justification for—academic and nonacademic support cuts.

Once the decisions are made, however, process is critical. Personal communication directly from deans or directors to those affected should be a top priority. Every effort should be made to personally accommodate as many affected staff and faculty as possible. Salary cuts, furloughs, reassignment, retraining, increased responsibilities, opportunities to move within the institution or system, career counseling, early retirement, buy-outs, and severance pay are all practices that can ease an otherwise horrific experience.

The point is to demonstrate that the institution *cares* about its staff and faculty despite the tough decisions it must make. Staff and faculty may not like the decisions that are made, but if they believe that their interests were defended, they were treated honestly and fairly, and they were consulted and listened to, the process will be less destructive than it might otherwise be.

Those who remain after a downsizing will be less demoralized and better able to regroup and commit themselves to quality work. It is important to remember that as relieved as those who remain are, they have probably been affected by the unknown and the anxiety of major institutional retrenchment or restructuring. They may have lost friends and important colleagues; they may find themselves in new positions with new responsibilities and new supervisors. One private institution, after undergoing reeling cuts to staff and faculty, sponsored a two-day mandatory retreat for all those still employed to focus on issues such as dealing with crisis, change, and stress; deepening trust and enhancing the quality of relationships; and defining vision and purpose. Such an effort will be resisted by some members of the staff and faculty (and begrudged as a needless expense); nonetheless, the institution needs to find ways to refocus, raise morale, and direct its attention to the future.

Loss of Credibility with the Public

Higher education's credibility with the public has eroded over a long period of time and there are no quick fixes. Neither does it fall to any one group to enhance the public image of higher education. Presidents need to do what presidents do, and that is, continually promote and advance the cause of their institution with the appropriate constituencies. There is much good news that could be featured about the accomplishments of those in higher education, and it is up to offices of public relations to pursue positive coverage daily. Higher education also would be well served by efforts to inform the public in community service spots on television and radio about questions of concern or misconceptions that the public may hold regarding higher education issues. Topics could include differences in mission among research universities, comprehensive institutions, liberal arts colleges, and community colleges; the purpose of tenure, including its roots in academic freedom and how it is earned; expectations for teaching, research, and service; or why institutions do not hire their own doctoral students. Such spots could be sponsored by the institution, faculty senates, unions, or other concerned groups. What is needed above and beyond these formal attempts at image building are the efforts of every member of the administrative staff and faculty.

One of the findings from the APT morale assessment was the importance of their external relations with the public. Positive external relations are a significant predictor of high morale for midlevel administrators. If they value their relationships with the public, they should be encouraged to nurture those relationships. Midlevel administrators are in direct contact with groups such as prospective students, parents, alumni, teachers, counselors, media representatives, employers, contractors, and vendors. Every administrator has neighbors, family, friends, and relatives. Midlevel administrators can serve as positive ambassadors on behalf of the university. To do so, however, they must feel good about the quality of their work lives and the place that they are employed. Every administrator who feels like an important member of the campus community and feels a common sense of purpose in supporting the academic mission, can foster a positive image of the university and dispel rumors and misunderstandings that abound in the public. Those who feel good about their jobs and their employers make good representatives on behalf of higher education.

Similarly, faculty members come into contact with the public in a variety of ways. The faculty morale assessment indicated that one source of negative morale for faculty is the reward structure for teaching and service. Many faculty agree with the public sentiment that the balance between research, teaching, and service is skewed and needs to be reexamined. Many are more committed to teaching, and teaching undergraduates specifically, than they are to research, but they often operate under a set of expectations where this commitment may be penalized. Teaching is a vital component of faculty members' responsibilities, no matter whether they are employed at a research university, a liberal arts college, or a community college. The emphasis and time spent will differ by institutional type, but it is no less important that teaching be well done at a research university than it is at a liberal arts college. Teaching and working with students are important to the vast majority of faculty members. They need to voice this commitment to those who would relegate teaching and concern for undergraduate education to second-class citizenship.

Even the emphasis on teaching is not enough if the public perceives higher education as a private benefit rather than a public good. We must actively demonstrate that higher education institutions serve the state in which they reside and the nation in general, not just those who earn degrees. Postsecondary education benefits society by supplying a better educated work force, which in turn increases the competitiveness of the nation. Besides the benefit of an educated citizenry, research also can have a direct benefit to the nation. Faculty need to help the public relations personnel spotlight those research projects that bring in external monies, generate jobs, or attract new industries.

Service may be the most underappreciated aspect of the faculty role. Many faculty serve their communities by applying their expertise to advise community groups, solve technical problems, testify before legislatures and juries, consult with business, industry, government agencies and private nonprofit groups, and conduct contracted research. Some of the work is voluntary and some of it is paid, but rarely is it recognized by the institutional reward structure. As a result, faculty, particularly untenured faculty, are warned not to spend too much time in service because it will not help them, and could hurt them, in the tenure review process. Ethnic and racial minority and women faculty are often in demand in their communities as role models, speakers, and to work with community groups on issues of gender, race, discrimination, access, and equality. These faculty have been penalized in the reward structure at the same time that their deans and chairs are encouraging them to be visible and often are showcasing them in public.

Higher education needs to reverse itself on the worth of service. One researcher, Ernest Boyer, is eloquent on the role of service in *Scholarship Reconsidered*, and a number of professional groups have begun to address the faculty role and the system of faculty rewards.[3] Rather than being nonconsequential in terms of the reward structure, service should be recognized as an important part of the faculty member's professional responsibility. Admittedly, not all faculty have expertise that is directly relevant to the public or in demand, but those who do should be encouraged to be visible and active in public service. Applying professional expertise to society's problems has never been more needed and higher education has never been so in need of the good will of the public it serves.

Senior administrators need to encourage faculty senates or other representative faculty groups to address the reward structure, especially the criteria for tenure and promotion, and make it congruent with institutional or school mission and faculty preference. Preferences may well vary among faculty, and some institutions are attempting to accommodate a variety of roles for faculty to pursue. Traditionally, faculty were expected to perform essentially the same tasks for their entire career. We are beginning to acknowledge that faculty interests may change with age and stage of development. That may mean that faculty would prefer to emphasize one aspect of their work over another at particular stages. Perhaps all faculty should be able to arrange multiple-year contracts that allow them to concentrate their energies in teaching for a period of time, then research, then service, for example. Or perhaps faculty wish to specialize in one aspect of their work. There may well be models of faculty work, other than the traditional model, that will better serve faculty, their institutions, and the public. It may be that there is nothing wrong with the traditional model of faculty work other than the fact that it has become skewed in practice. What may be needed is a simple return to tradition and the commitment to research, teaching, *and* service. Faculty are paying a high price in public trust for allowing the balance between their three work responsibilities to become skewed and it is time to renew our professional commitment to the public good.

Increased Internal Conflict

The conflict described as internal to colleges and universities is a function of the changing face of higher education. Campuses are not as homogenous as they once were. There is tension by rank among faculty and by seniority among administrators. There is tension between the sexes, the races and the ethnic groups, and this is true of students, administrators, and faculty. Debates over whom to admit, what to teach, and how it should be taught involve all sectors of the campus. Critical theorists and deconstructionists take on positivists and the scientific method. Faculty cannot even understand one another. Increased specialization of faculty means they have less in common with each other; the same phenomenon has created territorial divides between administrators who used to be generalists. And as usual, there is little mutual respect between administrators and faculty.

This portrayal may be harsh and may not apply to all campuses. Unfortunately, to some degree, it is true of many. With regard to morale assessments, midlevel administrators point to the lack of recognition and appreciation they receive for their efforts and complain about the inequities they perceive between their status and that of faculty. At the same time, positive relationships with faculty are clearly important to them. Similarly, faculty indicate that collegial relations are very important to their morale and they consistently express their displeasure with the increased number of administrators and the leadership they perceive from senior administrators. The lack of community is striking.

This generalization is not to suggest that there are not quality relationships between individual faculty, individual administrators, and between faculty and administrators. There are, but the quality of relationships in general is a cause for concern. Debate over issues of substance is healthy and vital to academe, but one hopes for informed debate that has as its purpose the pursuit of the common good. Campuses have come to be dominated by administrative empire-builders and faculty entrepreneurs who operate more from self-interest and less from a commitment to the academic mission of the institution. The many who would oppose these self-serving priorities have been silent. It is time to reaffirm our common goals and discover common ground from which we can rebuild the academic community.

Facing tough times can further undermine relationships as administrators and faculty protect their "turf," argue for their worth relative to others, and call for others to be cut. Or, facing tough times can be a catalyst for coming together. Once the decisions are made and implemented, those who remain must find ways to meet new expectations, to do more with less. There will be more committees, task forces, and work groups created to deal with new realities. As much as both staff and faculty in higher education disdain committees, they do serve the purpose of bringing people together who ordinarily do not interact with one another. When group members work together to solve a problem, they often gain a new respect for one another, they listen and learn that their differences are not so great, and, hopefully, that their goals and objectives are more in concert than not. There is worth in the spirited give and take of debating ideas and priorities and methods. There is also worth in identifying those common values that keep us committed to academe as a place to work. Those common values can supersede our differences and allow us as a campus community to move beyond conflict to mutual respect and support.

Final Thoughts

The specific suggestions in Chapter 10 are made in response to findings from one university. The best suggestions are those generated in the context they will be used. No two campuses will have the same specific issues, and yet there is remarkable consistency across campuses in the issues that concern midlevel administrators and faculty. The literature typically reflects those matters that will be important to most assessments. Conducting the assessment, however, identifies the priorities and the idiosyncrasies on a given campus. Whatever those are, they need in turn to be addressed by efforts that are specific to that campus. It is worth knowing what others have tried and what works elsewhere, but ultimately each campus needs to improve the climate and quality of its distinctive culture.

The situation on many campuses, for both midlevel administrators and faculty, is that morale is exceedingly low and these are exceedingly tough times to try to do anything about it. Optimally, we should not wait until times of crisis to worry about morale. We should attend to the quality of work life of staff and faculty, to the trust of the public, and the sense of community on campus long before the tough times arrive. We need high morale to sustain us through the tough times. And those campuses that have made the morale of their staff and faculty a priority will probably suffer less than those that have not, because they will be able to focus on maintaining the high morale they have. Nonetheless, every campus can begin to pay attention to quality of work life at any point it chooses. If times are tough, it is far better to begin immediately than to allow conditions to worsen.

Morale is important. Our morale is our commitment to move forward, our enthusiasm to take on new challenges, and our spirit to maintain the highest of standards and quality. Our academic institutions, the public that we serve, and particularly our students, deserve no less.

Notes

1. Harmon, S. 1995. "Look Inward for Budget Solutions." *AAHE Bulletin* 47 (10), p. 17.
2. Rhoades, G. 1995. "Rising Administrative Costs in Instructional Units." *Thought & Action* 9 (1), p. 7–24.
3. Boyer, E. L. 1990. *Scholarship Reconsidered: Priorities of the Professoriate*. Princeton, NJ: The Carnegie Foundation for the Advancement of Teaching.

APPENDIX 1: SAMPLE LETTERS

Sample Letter to Solicit Participation in Faculty Interviews

Dear Colleague,

As you may be aware, the University of Hawaii at Manoa Faculty Senate conducts a morale survey every two years to assess faculty's perceptions of a number of work-related issues. This year we are revising and updating the survey instrument in response to comments in the past. To do so, we are interviewing a number of faculty to identify concerns that we may have overlooked. We hope you will be willing to be interviewed about your experiences as a faculty member at Manoa.

Christine Des Jarlais, a graduate student in higher education, will be contacting you soon to arrange a time for the interview. We realize that your time is exceedingly valuable. The purpose of the interview is to identify items to be added to the survey instrument. We will ask you to talk about your experiences as a faculty member at University of Hawaii at Manoa and what aspects of your work life contribute positively or negatively to your morale.

The interview will last only one hour and will be scheduled at your convenience. We also want you to know that your comments will be held in absolute confidentiality. Your honest and candid responses are important to us and we want to assure you that we will not attribute any specific remarks to individuals.

Thank you in advance for your time and consideration of this request. Chris will be contacting you in the next few weeks to arrange a time to meet. In the meantime, if you have any questions regarding the interview, please call me at 956-4116.

Sincerely,

Linda K. Johnsrud, Chair
Manoa Faculty Senate Executive Committee

Sample Letter to Solicit Participation in Focus Groups of Midlevel Administrators

Dear Colleague,

As you may be aware, we are launching an effort on campus to assess the morale of midlevel admin-istrators. An advisory board has been formed and we are beginning plans for a large-scale survey to identify those work-related issues that have an effect on morale. To ensure that the survey asks the questions most relevant to this campus, we are holding a series of small-group sessions to hear directly from midlevel administrators.

We wish to invite you to participate in this phase as a member of a focus group. The purpose of focus groups is to identify issues that should be included in a large-scale survey. We ask individuals to talk about their experiences on campus and what aspects of their work lives contribute positively or negatively to their morale. Because focus groups provide for interaction on a topic rather than singu-lar responses, they tend to generate quite a bit of discussion that reminds participants of issues they might not otherwise recall.

The results of the group's interaction will be recorded and analyzed to help us identify the most important issues. Vicki J. Rosser, research assistant on the project, also will be present. We will discuss the importance of confidentiality with the participants before we begin so everyone can feel comfortable. We will, of course, keep all individual comments confidential.

We invite you to participate in a small group scheduled for:

Friday, November 7

Campus Center, Rm 301

2:00 pm - 4:00 pm

If you are interested and available, please call 956-4116 and leave a message letting us know that you will be attending. If you are not free at the scheduled time but would like to participate at another time, let us know and we will try to include you in another group.

We look forward to meeting with you.

Sincerely,

Linda K. Johnsrud
Principal Investigator

Sample Cover Letter for Survey of Midlevel Administrators

Dear University of Hawaii Colleague:

The attached confidential survey has been designed to examine morale among administrative, professional, and technical personnel (APT) at the University of Hawai'i. We hope this study will provide information that may affect program objectives to enhance the quality of work for current and future APTs.

We ask that you take the time to complete the enclosed questionnaire and provide us with your administrative experience at the university. You are assured of complete confidentiality. No individual names will ever be associated with individual responses. The coding that appears in the corner of your questionnaire is to enable us to send follow-up reminders to increase the response rate. The results of the study will be reported in broad patterns only and results will be made available to the university community.

Please make every effort to complete and return the questionnaire within one week of receiving it. Thank you in advance for your time and candor.

Sincerely,

Linda K. Johnsrud
Associate Professor, Higher Education

Mie Watanabe
Director of EEO & Affirmative Action

Peggy S. Hong
System Director of Human Resources

Sample Cover Letter for Survey of Faculty

Dear Colleague,

The Manoa Faculty Senate has conducted a survey of faculty morale every few years since 1983. This year the survey has been revamped to make it more representative of the concerns of all members of the faculty congress. The intent of the survey is to determine the current level of faculty morale and also to establish baseline data to track the changes in faculty morale over time.

This year it is especially important to assess faculty morale. We have a new president of the University of Hawaii System and chancellor of Manoa. We also are facing budget constraints that could have long-term consequences for Manoa faculty and the Manoa academic program. Your responses will help the senate in formulating recommendations to the administration.

You are assured of complete confidentiality. The coding that appears in the corner of your questionnaire is to enable us to send follow-up reminders to increase the response rate. No individual names will ever be associated with individual responses. Results will be reported in aggregate patterns only. Anecdotal comments will be stripped of identifiers.

Please make every effort to complete and return the questionnaire within one week of receiving it. We appreciate the importance of your time. The survey should not take more than 20 minutes to complete. Please take the time now to let us know how you feel about your current experience as a Manoa faculty member.

Sincerely,

Linda K. Johnsrud, Chair
Manoa Faculty Senate Executive Committee

Sample Follow-Up Letter #1 for Survey of Midlevel Administrators

Dear Colleague:

More than one week ago we mailed you a survey asking you to respond to a series of questions about your job at the University of Hawaii and its effect on your morale. If you have completed and returned your questionnaire, please disregard this letter and thank you for your help with this project. If not, please take the time now to provide us with your perceptions.

This study is being conducted because we believe that learning about your experiences will enable the University to enhance the quality of work life of APTs. We cannot overemphasize the importance each questionnaire has to the credibility of the results. For the results of this project to be truly representative of the interests and concerns of APTs, it is essential that each person return his or her questionnaire. Your response is greatly appreciated.

Sincerely,

Dr. Linda K. Johnsrud
Project Coordinator

Sample Follow-Up Letter #2 for Survey of Midlevel Administrators

Dear Colleague:

I am writing to you about our APT morale study. As of today we have not received your completed questionnaire.

The large number of questionnaires returned is very encouraging. But, whether we will be able to describe accurately the opinions of the APTs depends on you and others who have not yet responded. Past experience suggests that those of you who have not sent in your questionnaires may hold quite different opinions about the APT experience from those who have.

Some concern has been expressed about the confidentiality of the study. Let me personally assure you that your response is entirely confidential. No individual names will be associated with individual responses. The coding on the first mailing was to allow us to follow-up on nonrespondents. The demographic information requested will not be used to identify individuals but rather to determine whether the results differ by factors such as gender, race, age, campus, or work unit. The findings will be reported in the aggregate only.

The results of this study are important to our understanding of the quality of work life at the university for APTs. In the event that your questionnaire has been misplaced, a replacement is enclosed. I urge you to complete and return it as quickly as possible.

Your contribution to the success of this study is greatly appreciated.

Sincerely,

Dr. Linda K. Johnsrud
Project Coordinator

Sample Follow-Up Letter #1 for Survey of Faculty

Dear Colleague:

Nearly two weeks ago I wrote you seeking your participation in a morale study of faculty members at the University of Hawaii-Manoa. As of today we have not received your completed questionnaire.

We have undertaken this study because we believe that assessing morale will enable the Faculty Senate to work toward improving the quality of work lives of faculty. I am writing to you again because of the significance each questionnaire has to the usefulness of this study. For the results of this project to be truly representative of the interests of faculty, it is essential that each person return his or her questionnaire.

If you already have completed and returned your questionnaire, thank you. If not, please take the time now to provide us with your perceptions. Your response is greatly appreciated.

Sincerely,

Linda K. Johnsrud, Chair
Manoa Faculty Senate Executive Committee

Sample Follow-Up Letter #2 for Survey of Faculty

Dear Colleague:

I am writing to you about our study of faculty morale at the University of Hawaii-Manoa. As of today we have not received your completed questionnaire.

The large number of questionnaires returned is very encouraging. But, whether we will be able to describe accurately the morale of faculty depends on you and others who have not yet responded. Past experience suggests that those of you who have not sent in your questionnaires may have quite different experiences as faculty from those who have.

The results of this study are very important in guiding the Faculty Senate's efforts to improve the quality of the work lives of faculty at Manoa. In the event that your questionnaire has been misplaced, a replacement is enclosed. I urge you to complete it and return it as quickly as possible.

Your contribution to the success of this study is appreciated greatly.

Sincerely,

Linda K. Johnsrud, Chair
Manoa Faculty Senate Executive Committee

APPENDIX 2: SAMPLE SURVEY OF MID-LEVEL ADMINISTRATOR MORALE

This survey instrument has been developed to examine morale among mid-level administrators at the University. We define morale as a state of mind regarding one's job. It includes satisfaction, commitment, loyalty and a sense of common purpose

Please respond to each of the following work-related issues twice: first, indicate the extent of the importance of the issue to you by circling your response on a range of "1" to "5." For example, a response rate of "1" indicates that this issue is not important to you, and a response of "5" indicates that it is very important to you.

Second, indicate the nature of the issues's impact on your morale in your current work situation, either negative or positive. For example, a response of "-2" indicates that the issue has a negative impact upon your morale, and a response of "+2" indicates that it has a positive impact on your morale. A response of "0" indicates that the issue has no impact on your morale.

	I. How important are these issues to you?					II. What is the impact of these issues on your current morale?				
	Not Important	Some Importance		Very Important		Negative Impact		No Impact		Positive Impact
	1	2	3	4	5	-2	-1	0	+1	+2

Institutional Factors

1.	Support for professional activities	1	2	3	4	5	-2	-1	0	+1	+2
2.	Opportunity for career development	1	2	3	4	5	-2	-1	0	+1	+2
3.	Opportunity for promotions	1	2	3	4	5	-2	-1	0	+1	+2
4.	Clear performance criteria	1	2	3	4	5	-2	-1	0	+1	+2
5.	Hiring practices	1	2	3	4	5	-2	-1	0	+1	+2
6.	Hiring for external candidates	1	2	3	4	5	-2	-1	0	+1	+2
7.	Workload distribution	1	2	3	4	5	-2	-1	0	+1	+2
8.	Staff turnover	1	2	3	4	5	-2	-1	0	+1	+2
9.	Ethnic diversity of staff	1	2	3	4	5	-2	-1	0	+1	+2
10.	Gender diversity of staff	1	2	3	4	5	-2	-1	0	+1	+2
11.	Federal/State government mandates	1	2	3	4	5	-2	-1	0	+1	+2
12.	Bureaucratic red tape	1	2	3	4	5	-2	-1	0	+1	+2
13.	Institutional sex discrimination (subtle and/or overt)	1	2	3	4	5	-2	-1	0	+1	+2

	I. How important are these issues to you?			II. What is the impact of these issues on your current morale?	
	Not Important	Some Importance	Very Important	Negative Impact	No Impact	Positive Impact
	1	2 3 4	5	-2 -1	0 +1	+2

Institutional issues continued

14.	Institutional racial/ethnic discrimination (subtle and/or overt)	1	2 3 4	5	-2 -1	0 +1	+2
15.	Program reviews	1	2 3 4	5	-2 -1	0 +1	+2
16.	Budget reviews						
17.	Retirement plans/benefits	1	2 3 4	5	-2 -1	0 +1	+2
18.	Age discrimination	1	2 3 4	5	-2 -1	0 +1	+2
19.	Revenue/resources for your unit	1	2 3 4	5	-2 -1	0 +1	+2
20.	Parking	1	2 3 4	5	-2 -1	0 +1	+2
21.	Physical work environment	1	2 3 4	5	-2 -1	0 +1	+2
22.	Reputation of the University	1	2 3 4	5	-2 -1	0 +1	+2
23.	Ethical conduct in unit	1	2 3 4	5	-2 -1	0 +1	+2
24.	Salary	1	2 3 4	5	-2 -1	0 +1	+2

Professional factors

25.	Relationship with faculty	1	2 3 4	5	-2 -1	0 +1	+2
26.	Relationship with students	1	2 3 4	5	-2 -1	0 +1	+2
27.	Relationship with the public	1	2 3 4	5	-2 -1	0 +1	+2
28.	Relationship with sr. administrators	1	2 3 4	5	-2 -1	0 +1	+2
29.	Degree of trust from supervisor	1	2 3 4	5	-2 -1	0 +1	+2
30.	Recognition for expertise	1	2 3 4	5	-2 -1	0 +1	+2
31.	Recognition for contribution	1	2 3 4	5	-2 -1	0 +1	+2
32.	Sufficient guidance	1	2 3 4	5	-2 -1	0 +1	+2
33.	Pressures to perform	1	2 3 4	5	-2 -1	0 +1	+2
34.	Communication from supervisors	1	2 3 4	5	-2 -1	0 +1	+2

	Not Important	Some Importance			Very Important	Negative Impact		No Impact		Positive Impact
35. Communication between units	1	2	3	4	5	-2	-1	0	+1	+2
36. Importance of my job to institution	1	2	3	4	5	-2	-1	0	+1	+2
37. Co-workers performance	1	2	3	4	5	-2	-1	0	+1	+2
38. Within departmental relationships	1	2	3	4	5	-2	-1	0	+1	+2
39. Cross-department relations	1	2	3	4	5	-2	-1	0	+1	+2
40. Sense of teamwork	1	2	3	4	5	-2	-1	0	+1	+2
41. Racial/ethnic harassment	1	2	3	4	5	-2	-1	0	+1	+2
42. Sexual harassment	1	2	3	4	5	-2	-1	0	+1	+2
43. Department politics	1	2	3	4	5	-2	-1	0	+1	+2
44. Availability of mentoring	1	2	3	4	5	-2	-1	0	+1	+2
45. Feedback to performance	1	2	3	4	5	-2	-1	0	+1	+2
46. Authority to make decisions	1	2	3	4	5	-2	-1	0	+1	+2
47. Support of collective bargaining unit	1	2	3	4	5	-2	-1	0	+1	+2
48. Visibility in the organization	1	2	3	4	5	-2	-1	0	+1	+2
49. Leadership of your unit	1	2	3	4	5	-2	-1	0	+1	+2
50. Institutional leadership	1	2	3	4	5	-2	-1	0	+1	+2

Please indicate your agreement with the following statements about your work.

	Strongly Disagree				Strongly Agree
51. There is too little variety in my job.	-2	-1	0	+1	+2
52. There's a common purpose in my unit.	-2	-1	0	+1	+2
53. There must be better places to work.	-2	-1	0	+1	+2
54. I would like more freedom on the job.	-2	-1	0	+1	+2
55. I am satisfied with the work I do.	-2	-1	0	+1	+2

Please indicate your agreement with the following statements about the institution.

		Strongly Disagree			Strongly Agree	
56.	I am loyal to the institution.	-2	-1	0	+1	+2
57.	My opinions are valued.	-2	-1	0	+1	+2
58.	This institution values its employees.	-2	-1	0	+1	+2
59.	This institution is a caring organization.	-2	-1	0	+1	+2
60.	This is a fair institution.	-2	-1	0	+1	+2

61. Please indicate your level of morale with respect to your experience on your campus.

Low morale				High morale
1	2	3	4	5

62. Do you have plans to leave your current position?   Yes_____   No_____

63. Do you feel "stuck" in your position?   Yes_____   No_____

Demographic information

64. What years have you been employed on your campus?   19_____ to 19_____

65. Which of the following most closely describes your administrative unit?

Academic Affairs _____   External Affairs _____
Student Affairs _____   Other (please specify) _____
Business/Facilities Affairs _____   _____

66. Please state the title of your position/job: _____
67. What is your pay range? (01-17) _____

68. What is your gender?   Female_____   Male_____

69. What is the year of your birth?   _____

70. What is your race/ethnicity? (indicate group with which you most closely identify): _____

What kind of staff development or training would be most helpful to you?

_____

Please feel free to provide any additional comments on the back of this page.

THANK YOU FOR YOUR TIME AND EFFORT!

APPENDIX 3:

SAMPLE SURVEY OF UNIVERSITY FACULTY MORALE

This survey instrument has been developed to examine morale among faculty at the University. We define morale as a state of mind regarding one's worklife. Morale includes satisfaction, commitment, loyalty and a sense of common purpose.

Please indicate the extent to which each of the following factors contribute to your morale by circling the appropriate number. For example, a response of "-2" indicates that this factor has negative impact on your morale. A response of "+2" indicates that this factor has a positive impact on your morale. A response of "0" indicates that the issue has no impact on your morale. Circling NA indicates that the factor is not applicable to you personally.

Please rate the following factors in terms of their impact on your morale:

	Negative Impact		No Impact		Positive Impact	
	-2	-1	0	+1	+2	NA
Professional worklife						
1. Undergraduate teaching load	-2	-1	0	+1	+2	NA
2. Graduate teaching load	-2	-1	0	+1	+2	NA
3. Committee load	-2	-1	0	+1	+2	NA
4. Advising load	-2	-1	0	+1	+2	NA
5. Service to the university	-2	-1	0	+1	+2	NA
6. Service to the community	-2	-1	0	+1	+2	NA
7. Consulting opportunities	-2	-1	0	+1	+2	NA
8. Support for professional travel	-2	-1	0	+1	+2	NA
9. Availability of graduate assistants	-2	-1	0	+1	+2	NA
10. Clerical support	-2	-1	0	+1	+2	NA
11. Access to institutional research funds	-2	-1	0	+1	+2	NA
12. Access to extramural research funds	-2	-1	0	+1	+2	NA
13. Institutional research support	-2	-1	0	+1	+2	NA
14. Physical work environment	-2	-1	0	+1	+2	NA
15. Parking	-2	-1	0	+1	+2	NA
16. Reputation of the University	-2	-1	0	+1	+2	NA
Reward/evaluation system						
17. Institutional rewards for teaching	-2	-1	0	+1	+2	NA
18. Institutional rewards for research	-2	-1	0	+1	+2	NA
19. Institutional rewards for service	-2	-1	0	+1	+2	NA
20. Feedback at contract renewal	-2	-1	0	+1	+2	NA
21. Tenure process	-2	-1	0	+1	+2	NA
22. Promotion process	-2	-1	0	+1	+2	NA
23. Post-tenure review process	-2	-1	0	+1	+2	NA

Please rate the following factors in terms of their impact on your morale:

	Negative Impact		No Impact		Positive Impact	

Collegial relations

24. Relations with department chair	-2	-1	0	+1	+2	NA
25. Support for career from chair	-2	-I	0	+I	+2	NA
26. Social fit with department	-2	-1	0	+1	+2	NA
27. Intellectual fit with department	-2	-1	0	+1	+2	NA
28. Collegial relations within department	-2	-1	0	+1	+2	NA
29. Collegiality among University faculty	-2	-1	0	+1	+2	NA

Students

30. Enthusiasm of undergraduate students	-2	-1	0	+1	+2	NA
31. Enthusiasm of graduate students	-2	-1	0	+1	+2	NA
32. Ability of undergraduate students	-2	-1	0	+1	+2	NA
33. Ability of graduate students	-2	-1	0	+1	+2	NA
34. Institutional support of undergraduates	-2	-1	0	+1	+2	NA
35. Institutional support of graduate students	-2	-1	0	+1	+2	NA

Faculty Governance

Faculty input in department level:

36. • academic decisions	-2	-1	0	+1	+2	NA
37. • budget decisions	-2	-1	0	+1	+2	NA
38. • personnel decisions	-2	-1	0	+1	+2	NA

Faculty input in college/unit level:

39. • academic decisions	-2	-1	0	+1	+2	NA
40. • budget decisions	-2	-1	0	+1	+2	NA
41. • personnel decisions	-2	-1	0	+1	+2	NA

Faculty input in university level:

42. • academic decisions	-2	-1	0	+1	+2	NA
43. • budget decisions	-2	-1	0	+1	+2	NA
44. • personnel decisions	-2	-1	0	+1	+2	NA
45. Protection of academic freedom	-2	-1	0	+1	+2	NA

Personal Factors

46. Housing	-2	-1	0	+1	+2	NA
47. Standard of living	-2	-1	0	+1	+2	NA
48. Current salary	-2	-1	0	+1	+2	NA
49. Fringe benefits	-2	-1	0	+1	+2	NA
50. Retirement benefits	-2	-1	0	+1	+2	NA
51. Professional mobility	-2	-1	0	+1	+2	NA

Please take a moment to review the factors 1-51 listed, and

• List three of these factors (or others) that have the most negative impact on your morale.

1._____ 2._____ 3._____

Please take a moment to review the factors 1-51 listed, and

• List three of these factors (or others) that have the most positive impact on your morale.

1._____ 2._____ 3._____

Please rate the following factors in terms of their impact on your ability to function effectively:

	Negative Impact		No Impact		Positive Impact	
52. Library	-2	-1	0	+1	+2	NA
53. Office of Research Administration	-2	-1	0	+1	+2	NA
54. Office of Faculty Dev/Academic Support	-2	-1	0	+1	+2	NA
55. Facilities (repair & maintenance)	-2	-1	0	+1	+2	NA
56. Computing facilities	-2	-1	0	+1	+2	NA

Please respond to each of the following on a 5 point scale, from weak to strong in the first section, from low to high confidence in the second. Circling "3" indicates a midpoint on each continuum.

Please rate the way you view the advocacy for University faculty by:

	Weak				Strong	
57. Your Chair	1	2	3	4	5	NA
58. Your Dean/Director	1	2	3	4	5	NA
58. Central Administration	1	2	3	4	5	NA
60. University President	1	2	3	4	5	NA
61. Board of Regents	1	2	3	4	5	NA
62. Legislature	1	2	3	4	5	NA
63. Governor	1	2	3	4	5	NA
64. Community	1	2	3	4	5	NA
65. Faculty Senate	1	2	3	4	5	NA
66. Collective Bargaining Unit	1	2	3	4	5	NA

Please rate the confidence you have in the leadership exhibited by:

	Low Confidence				High Confidence	
67. Your Chair	1	2	3	4	5	NA
68. Your Dean/Director	1	2	3	4	5	NA
69. Central Administration	1	2	3	4	5	NA
70. University President	1	2	3	4	5	NA
71. Board of Regents	1	2	3	4	5	NA
72. Faculty Senate Exec. Committee	1	2	3	4	5	NA
73. Collective Bargaining Unit	1	2	3	4	5	NA

Please indicate the extent of your agreement with each of the following statements. A response of "-2" indicates strong disagreement and "+2" indicates strong agreement. Circling "0" indicates a neutral response.

	Strongly Disagree		Neutral		Strongly Agree
74. I enjoy the variety in my work.	-2	-1	0	+1	+2
75. There's a common purpose in my unit.	-2	-1	0	+1	+2
76. I am enthusiastic about my work.	-2	-1	0	+1	+2
77. I have sufficient autonomy in my work.	-2	-1	0	+1	+2
78. I am satisfied with the work I do.	-2	-1	0	+1	+2

Please indicate your agreement with the following statements about the institution.

	Strongly Disagree		Neutral		Strongly Agree
79. I am loyal to this institution.	-2	-1	0	+1	+2
80. My opinions are valued.	-2	-1	0	+1	+2
81. This institution values its employees.	-2	-1	0	+1	+2
82. This institution is a caring organization.	-2	-1	0	+1	+2
83. This is a fair institution.	-2	-1	0	+1	+2

Please indicate your level of morale with respect to your experience on your campus.

	Low Morale				High Morale
	1	2	3	4	5

Demographic Information

Lastly (you are almost finished!), please answer the following items so that we may make a more informed interpretation of the data.

Number of years on the University Faculty?   _____

Demographics continued

Faculty classification: How is your appointment categorized?

Instructional	_____
Researcher	_____
Specialist	_____
Librarian	_____
Agent	_____
Other	_____
Split appointment (please specify)	_____

Age (please check one)   _____ 22-35
                                                _____ 36-45
                                                _____ 46-55
                                                _____ 56-65
                                                _____   65+

Gender   _____ Female
                                                _____ Male

Race/Ethnicity (please indicate group with which you most closely identify):

                              _____

_____
Feel free to add any other comments.

Please return this survey in the enclosed envelope to:

                    THANK YOU VERY MUCH FOR YOUR TIME AND EFFORT.
                    YOUR PARTICIPATION IS GREATLY APPRECIATED.